W9-BZA-650

KAUAI RESTAURANTS AND DINING

WITH PRINCEVILLE AND POIPU BEACH

INTIMATE BISTROS · CULINARY ADVENTURES · BEACH BARS
FINE DINING · WATERFRONT RESTAURANTS · LOCAL DIVES
COFFEE SHOPS · ROMANTIC HIDEAWAYS · BUDGET FINDS
CASUAL SPOTS · HOLE-IN-THE-WALLS · ETHNIC EATERIES

HAWAII RESTAURANT GUIDE SERIES

ROBERT & CINDY CARPENTER

REVISED EDITION

KAUAI RESTAURANTS AND DINING
WITH PRINCEVILLE AND POIPU BEACH

1st Edition, Revised

ISBN-10 1-931752-37-0

ISBN-13 978-1-931752-37-4

Library of Congress Control Number: 2006910106

Printed in the United States of America

Holiday Publishing Inc.
Post Office Box 11120
Lahaina, HI 96761

holidaypublishing@yahoo.com

www.hawaiirestaurantguide.com

KAUAI RESTAURANTS AND DINING
WITH PRINCEVILLE AND POIPU BEACH

TABLE OF CONTENTS

Introduction

Pundits say that there are those who eat to live and those that live to eat. Since you're reading this you probably already have a leaning toward the latter group. Well, join the club! Food has taken on an importance never seen before. That's not to say that Mom's cooking wasn't good. What better place can you think of to develop your own sense for comfort food than at the kitchen table? However, with restaurants popping up on every corner and 24 hours of food shows airing daily, culinary pursuits have definitely come of age.

Hawaii is the perfect place to explore this newfound enthusiasm. In the islands you'll find people from around the world blending and sharing the best of their cultures. Naturally the local dining scene reflects this international view where noodle shops and Continental dining venues make perfect neighbors. Then, just to make things more interesting Hawaii people like to include some neo-fusion cuisine and contemporary sushi to complete the neighborhood mix.

This book was written in an attempt to define this wonderful disarray. Knowing full well that this was a nigh on impossible task we took off happily into the fog and aren't quite sure if we've emerged yet! Let's just say that six islands, seven years and 1500 dissimilar restaurants, ethnic eateries and hole-in-the-walls later you now have in your hands a copy of Kauai Restaurants and Dining.

Along the path of creation we found ourselves continually testing the envelope. Before putting pen to paper there first came research, which of course was our favorite part of the undertaking! Being self-confessed culinary vagabonds what better way to combine vices than by taking a dining junket across the Hawaiian Islands? As the adventure continued it started taking on a Keseyian spin. When the term "fusion confusion" entered our daily vocabulary we knew the time had arrived to develop a master criterion. Here's what we determined:

Experience has taught us that adventurous travelers like to be empowered. They don't care for travel experiences that include being shoved on a bus and handed a meal voucher. Nor do they like to be led around to all the standard guidebook hot spots. No, they want to go it alone and make their own decisions whenever possible. It became our goal to provide the support material required to do so.

To begin with people need to have accurate information concerning the physical location, website address, phone number, hours of operation, dress code, style of cuisine, credit cards and price range of each establishment. Then they like to see actual menu items with prices to determine budgeting. What might be a medium priced place to one person could be something entirely different to another!

Our restaurant selection process follows suit. We decided early on not to waste time writing about places we wouldn't bother revisiting and skipped right over to creating an A list. Why waste time beating up on also-rans when there are so many wonderful places to talk about? The results have been assembled into a collection that covers a range of tastes and styles from elegant to elemental.

Of course no restaurant guide would be complete without impressions. People have repeatedly told us that they want to know what to expect before they arrive. This can run the gamut from finding a parking place to personal preferences like waterfront dining. In our comment sections we try to deal with real world issues and leave the chamber of commerce spin to the paid inclusion publishers.

Finally, all of this was done at our own expense. Too much of what vacationers encounter is biased by compensation. In the realm of travel payola is offered in many forms. It could be through a free cruise, complimentary meals or outright cash payment. Regardless, the resulting work becomes an advertorial instead of an honest review. It's hard to be objective when they roll out the red carpet!

This brings us to the bane of all restaurant writers - timeliness. The travel world is constantly changing and no part changes faster than menus. Restaurateurs all seem to have revolving doors on their operations! So was creating this work an act of futility? We think not. Looking back over the last decade we see far more continuity than interruption.

It's our hope that you will enjoy this guide as a travelogue rather than consign it to the dusty reference shelf. Think of it as a personal journal and it will take you far. Life isn't perfect and neither is this book. Sure, a certain dish you spotted in a review may no longer be offered, but ask about the new special on the current menu and stretch your horizons. Isn't that why you came here in the first place?

And what if a stop turns out to be a complete catastrophe? Do what we do and laugh! When the host greets us with, "Hope you're not trying to catch a plane." Our standard response is, "Welcome to the islands!" Even the best restaurants have off-days. Chefs go on vacations like everyone else so maintain a positive attitude and major inconveniences will later seem like minor footnotes.

Enjoy your visit to Kauai. Explore the renowned sights and sounds found in the islands. But while you're here be sure to set time aside to discover the culturally diverse culinary experiences unique to America's Pacific Paradise!

Robert & Cindy Carpenter
Authors

Old Haunts

People ask us all sorts of questions, but "Is the local drive-in still open?" ranks near the top. This comes as no surprise as the restaurant business is well-known for its low margins and high mortality. Like everywhere else Kauai restaurants come and go. A tourism based economy might sound like a ticket to prosperity, but consider the challenges posed by size and distance. Combine a small market with 2500 miles of ocean and everything involved with business gets pricey.

We've decided to start this work by acknowledging some old favorites that have stepped to the sidelines. If your travels brought you to Kauai during the past ten years you may recognize a name or two. Otherwise, understand that many good times were had by those fortunate enough to remember these places:

A Pacific Café	Kapa'a
Aromas	Nawiliwili
Blossoming Lotus	Kapa'a
Camp House Grill	Kalaheo & Kapa'a
Coconuts	Kapa'a
Dali Deli / Café Cara	Koloa
Green Garden	Hanapepe
House of Seafood	Poipu
Taqueria Norteños	Koloa
Zelo's Beach House	Hanalei

That brings us to the next group of suspects. Long time Kauai people remember the island before mill closings and hurricanes changed its face. Those were years of colorful entrepreneurs and restaurants whose time has now passed. See if any of the following strikes a chord in your memory banks:

Charo's	Haena
Club Jetty	Nawiliwili
Hale Kapa	Princeville
Inn on the Cliffs	Lihue
Koloa Broiler	Koloa
Mike's Café	Hanapepe
Prince Bill's	Nawiliwili
Seashell	Wailua
Tamarind	Poipu
The Coconut Palace	Wailua

If this is your first visit to Kauai and you're afraid you missed all the excitement don't worry. In the islands once a location becomes a restaurant spot it's always a restaurant spot. Hang around awhile and you'll discover that the booth you're in may have once been occupied by Elvis and that before the Pacific Rim craze the place served Chinese! So get full value out of your stay by enjoying all that follows and discovering your own collection of old haunts.

Getting Around

At some point in their stay most adventurous Kauai visitors rent a car and take off on a road trip. This is a great way to see the sights, but before you start the engine there are a few things you should know. To begin with, unless you've been on the island before you'll probably need directions at some point. There are three distinctly different ways you'll find this done.

When you need help expect all of the following and often in combination:

1) The Mainland Method – ie, maps using route numbers, "Highway 56"

2) The Island Method – ie, signs using highway names, "Kuhio Highway"

3) The Local Method – ie, verbal using landmarks, "Go Donkey Beach"

Mainland visitors talk about going east or west. In the islands locals might say "Go Hanapepe" or "Go Lihue". Then, when directions do include a compass reference it's usually "Go North Side." On Kauai this could also be said as "Go Hanalei Side". Expect multiple references in verbal directions. The locals may not remember the route number, but they will know the town and destination.

Hawaii limits signage of all types to protect vistas. The signs that are permitted are physically small to deal with wind. In order to better get around determine the route number, name of the highway and your town and destination before starting out. If you get confused pull off the road to look at maps. Don't try to navigate and drive. Safety demands your full attention on the road and traffic.

The roads reflect the island territorial heritage. They follow geographical limits like shorelines rather than grids. Many have narrow right-of-ways and almost no shoulders. In remote areas one-lane bridges are common. The government has updated these roads, but physical realities restrict what can be done. Meanwhile some resist major changes to protect the old way of life and curb development.

If you get lost don't panic - you won't end up in Bangalore. When you're on an island and keep driving in the same direction you usually go all the way around and end up back in the same spot. That is, of course, except on Kauai where the circle island road was never completed! Obey the rules of the road - don't put everyone at risk by pulling an unplanned u-turn at a busy intersection.

Finally, remember that you're not the only one out there that's a bit perplexed. Hawaii has residents and visitors from all over the world. If you expect to see just about anything happen you won't be disappointed. Let your passengers do the sightseeing. If somebody spots a spouting whale or beautiful waterfall pull over and enjoy the scene. Always drive akamai and have a safe stay on Kauai!

Personal Favorites

He Said...She Said...We Said...

If there's something everyone wants to know it has to be, "What's your favorite restaurant?" That's a hard one to answer. There are dozens of great dining spots on Kauai. Nevertheless, just like beauty is in the eye of the beholder, individual tastes and preferences mean everything when making this call. Having said that we have decided to hold up the bulls-eye and offer our list of personal favorites:

Bakery

He Said...	She Said...	We Said...
Kilauea Bakery	Kilauea Bakery	Kilauea Bakery

Burgers

He Said...	She Said...	We Said...
Duane's Ono-Char	Hanalei Gourmet	Hanalei Gourmet

Pizza

He Said...	She Said...	We Said...
Pizzetta	Brick Oven	Pizzetta

Seafood

He Said...	She Said...	We Said...
Fish Express	Hanalei Dolphin	Wahooo

Steak

He Said...	She Said...	We Said...
Kalaheo Steak House	Wrangler's	CJ's

Sushi

He Said...	She Said...	We Said...
Sushi Bushido	Sushi Bushido	Sushi Bushido

Tacos

He Said...	She Said...	We Said...
Tropical Taco	ver'de	LaBamba

Tapas

He Said...	She Said...	We Said...
Bar Acuda	Bar Acuda	Bar Acuda

Category	He Said...	She Said...	We Said...
Asian	Mema Thai	King & I	Restaurant Kintaro
Budget	Da Imu Hut	Kalapaki Beach Hut	Hong Kong Café
Exotic	Pacific Island Bistro	Casablanca	Lemongrass Grill
Family	The Eggbert's	The Eggbert's	The Eggbert's
Fusion	Plantation Gardens	Hukilau Lanai	Roy's
Healthy	Hanapepe Café	Mermaids Café	Postcards
Island	Tip Top Cafe	Da Imu Hut	Lihue Barbecue Inn
Local	Hamura's	Hamura's	Hamura's
Romantic	Tidepools	Café Portofino	Plantation Gardens
Views	Dondero's	Café Portofino	Mediterranean Gourmet
Waterfront	Brennecke's	Mediterranean Gourmet	Beach House

Family Friendly

Dining out was once reserved for business gatherings and special occasions. If someone wasn't getting married the kids stayed at home. Today, family outings to favorite restaurants have become a universal pastime. Likewise, travel is more democratic with everyone in the household participating. This brings us to every parent's dilemma, "Where do we eat when we're so far from home?"

We decided to develop a list of places we could recommend to families visiting Kauai. Before making these selections we had to create a yardstick. Everything in the islands has its own spin, so naturally what constitutes family friendly has to be determined by looking through an island lens. So ditch the rules of proper behavior as proscribed by mainland morality and get on board!

To begin with, if mom, pop and the kids are all going to Kauai there are a bunch of plane tickets to buy. Then, since the Hawaiian Islands are in the middle of the Pacific Ocean those tickets are going to be expensive. Take that and add the cost of lodging and dad's wallet is probably going to be on life support. So the first rule we adopted was our selections had to be affordable.

Then we determined that since adult beverages are routinely available across the islands we would include places where they are served. Who cares what they are drinking at the next table? If you don't care to participate don't order anything! Smoking is banned in Hawaiian restaurants so that issue is moot. Add fun food and a relaxed atmosphere and you have the following recommendations:

Brick Oven Pizza	Kalaheo
Da Imu Hut Café	Hanapepe
Dani's Restaurant	Lihue
Duane's Ono-Char Burger	Anahola
Garden Island Barbecue	Lihue
Grind's Café & Espresso	Hanapepe
Hong Kong Café	Kapa'a
Joe's On The Green	Poipu
Kalaheo Café & Coffee Co	Kalaheo
Kalapaki Beach Hut	Lihue
Kountry Style Kitchen	Kapa'a
LaBamba Mexican Restaurant	Lihue
Lihue Barbecue Inn	Lihue
Pacific Pizza & Deli	Waimea
Pizzetta	Koloa & Kapa'a
Puka Dog	Poipu
Scotty's Beachside BBQ	Kapa'a
The Eggbert's	Kapa'a
The Hanalei Gourmet	Hanalei
Tomkats Grille	Koloa

Luau Shows

Luaus are an integral part of the ancient Hawaiian culture. Today's visitors have the opportunity to attend luau shows that combine dining and entertainment on a scale only the Kamehamehas would have recognized. These extravagant events are usually limited to a few nights a week and come in a number of packages so we've chosen to list them and suggest that you contact the providers and ask for current relevant details. It's best to reserve in advance as many luaus book solid.

Surf to Sunset Luau — Poipu Beach
Sheraton Kauai Resort
2440 Hoonani Road
Koloa, HI 96756
808-742-8200

Grand Hyatt Kauai Luau — Poipu Beach
Grand Hyatt Kauai Resort & Spa
1571 Poipu Road
Koloa, HI 96756
808-742-1234

Smith Family Garden Luau — Wailua River
Smith's Tropical Paradise
174 Wailua Road
Kapa'a, HI 96746
808-821-6895

Hiva Pasefika Luau — Coconut Grove
ResortQuest Kauai Beach at Makaiwa
650 Aleka Loop
Kapa'a, HI 96746
808-822-3455

Pa'ina 'O Hanalei Luau — North Shore
Princeville Resort
5520 Ka Haku Road
Princeville, HI 96722
808-826-2788

Luau Kilohana — Kilohana Plantation
Gaylord's at Kilohana
3-2087 Kaumualii Hwy (Hwy 50)
Lihue, HI 96766
808-245-9593

Watering Holes

Alcohol plays an interesting part in Hawaiian history. The missionaries abhorred it, the whalers wallowed in it and the rest of the population pretty much ignored it. Those who couldn't deal with alcohol are gone which leaves Hawaii squarely in the hands of people who don't see it as such a big deal. As a result beer, wine and assorted adult beverages are common features on menus across the islands.

Knowing that there are times when nothing else will do we would like to present a short list of possibilities. Understand that these are respectable establishments, they just so happen to have more of a focus on the good life than some others. If your minimal daily requirements include a cocktail hour you should feel right at home. Whether it's a quick drink or an evening's outing consider the following:

Bar Acuda	Hanalei
Brennecke's Beach Broiler	Poipu
Casablanca at Kiahuna	Poipu
CJ's Steak & Seafood	Princeville
Duke's Barefoot Bar	Nawiliwili
JJ's Broiler	Lihue
Kalypso Island Bar & Grill	Hanalei
Kauai Hula Girl Bar & Grill	Kapa'a
Keoki's Paradise	Poipu
Lizard Lounge Bar & Grill	Kapa'a
Pizzetta	Koloa & Kapa'a
Poipu Bay Grill & Bar	Poipu
Rob's Good Times Grill	Lihue
Stevenson's Library	Poipu
Saffron	Princeville
Sushi Blues	Hanalei
The Hanalei Gourmet	Hanalei
The Point	Poipu
Tradewinds	Kapa'a
Waimea Brew Pub	Waimea

Before going out on the island be aware that mixed drinks are often served weak. This is especially true at luaus where the complimentary punch is usually longer on juice then "punch". Then to add insult to injury somebody forgot to tell many of the proprietors that people really CAN tell the difference between good liquor and cheap booze. Ask what's in the well – quality call pours cost very little more.

So make your visit to Kauai whatever you want it to be. Everything has a proper time, and if it's adult time kick back and enjoy the good feelings, good food and good companionship. Just remember to have that really big night within walking distance of your hotel or with transportation provided by a designated driver. If good sense and all else fails remember that cabs are a lot cheaper than attorneys!

Quirks & Caveats

The farther one gets from something's origin the more likely it will take on a new identity. Since Hawaii is both geographically and culturally remote you can imagine the unique spins to be found in the islands. This shows up in all aspects of daily life but especially at the dinner table.

Let's start off with that ubiquitous condiment commonly known as soy sauce. In Hawaii soy sauce is called shoyu per the Japanese fashion. But wait, that doesn't mean that the Japanese version of soy sauce is preferred in Hawaii. No, the local taste runs to a lighter, sweeter product widely sold under the Aloha Shoyu label.

Like the Japanese, Hawaii people enjoy making teriyaki marinade with shoyu. Once again tastes change the recipe. In Japan teriyaki is a simple blend of soy sauce, rice wine and sugar, but in Hawaii the local Korean influence kicks in through the addition of green onions, garlic and ginger.

This takes us on to what constitutes salad. Mainland people have come to expect a combination of fresh vegetables and lettuces in their salads. That's not always the case in Hawaii. If the menu reads "toss salad" you can expect something you might recognize. However, if it reads "green salad" it probably means your meal comes with shredded cabbage while "salad" says get ready for mac and mayo.

Local tastes have put their stamp on meat dishes as well. Most Hawaii residents have Asian ancestry so those preferences naturally appear in entrees across the state. Choices like duck and lamb are common on Hawaiian menus along with finfish of every description. On a lesser note boneless, skinless, chicken thighs hold forth in a thousand incarnations, some quite good, others best left alone.

Let's not forget red meat. Hawaii people are fond of beef and pork. A whole hog cooked imu style is everybody's favorite. But understand that this is a fatty dish which underscores the local taste for fat. You'll see fat everywhere from the top of a piece of Katsu chicken to the belly of a prime ahi tuna. Like anything fat is OK in moderation, but unless you want to live and look local pass some of it by.

As you travel about you'll see "barbeque" wherever you go. This doesn't mean what you might think. In most cases Hawaii barbeque is flame grilled, teriyaki marinated meat. Unlike mainland barbeque brush-on sauces, rubs and smoke don't enter in. That doesn't mean it isn't good, it just means it's different.

Finally, let's touch on an all important issue. In short, "Where's the restroom?" Like everything else in the islands the answer can be a little different. Of course the better places usually have excellent facilities, but when you decide to hit the strip malls and mom-and-pops anything becomes possible. If your quest takes you through the kitchen just say, "Hi!" and consider it part of the adventure.

Legend

Dress Code and Restaurant Price Symbols are based upon dinner. Lunch is usually a less expensive meal during which more casual attire is acceptable.

Restaurant Prices:

$	<$10
$$	$10-$25
$$$	$25-$40
$$$$	$40+

Credit Cards Accepted:

AE	American Express
CB	Carte Blanche
DC	Diners Club
DIS	Discover
JCB	Japan Credit Bank
MC	Master Card
V	Visa

Days of Operation:

Su	Sunday
Mo	Monday
Tu	Tuesday
We	Wednesday
Th	Thursday
Fr	Friday
Sa	Saturday
X	Except

Example: XMo = Every Day Except Monday

Dress Code:

Casual	t shirts, shorts, flip-flops, baseball hats
Resort Casual	shirt with a collar, shorts with pockets, sandals
Evening Aloha	long pants on gentlemen with closed-toed shoes
Formal	long sleeved dress shirt or jacket for gentlemen
Note:	Bathing suits and tank tops are suitable attire on the beach and by the pool. Cover-ups are a must at even the most casual of dining spots.

Rating System:

✓	Good	Meets acceptable standards
✓✓	Better	Exceeds usual requirements
✓✓✓	Superior	Great choice in most areas
✓✓✓✓	Excellent	Often the best to be found
✓✓✓✓✓	Exceptional	Rare and unique experience

In Hawaii it's considered poor manners to speak badly of someone. As the locals tell their children, "No talk stink!" With that in mind we resolved to avoid using negatives commonly associated with restaurant reviews. This put us on the high road of only including places we would return to and leaving out the rest. After that came the challenge of sorting out our newfound A list on a numerical scale.

We looked at several different approaches before settling on a five point system that allowed flexibility without bogging us down. Within this structure we view the four major factors of food, service, ambiance and value as equally important and scored accordingly. After comparing the establishments on our list with one another ratings were given creating what we hope is an accurate overall picture.

Menu Items:

Nothing in the world of travel changes faster than restaurant menus. Everything from the seasonal availability of local produce to which side of the bed the chef got up on impacts what you're offered when you sit down to dine. Nowhere will you find this more true than in Hawaii where the fresh catch of the day normally IS caught that day. If the boats didn't bring in opakapaka it just isn't available.

This guide attempts to help the reader come to his own conclusions. Menu items were chosen to give a well-rounded cross-section of the prospects and a sense of depth and complexity. Signature dishes have been included whenever offered as they tend to be constants and represent the chef's expertise and direction. Actual menu descriptions are used to best convey the mood and feel diners can expect.

Reservations:

It is always wise to call ahead as even the most established restaurateurs realign their meal service and hours periodically. Changes can almost be guaranteed in vacation destinations like Hawaii where life itself revolves around the seasons.

Spelling, Punctuation, & Pricing:

We have duplicated the spelling, punctuation and pricing as printed on menus in use at the time of publication. If you think some of them are unusual you should have seen what they did to our computer spell check and grammar programs! As prices are subject to change at anytime they should only be used as guidelines.

Hawaiian Islands

ISLAND CUISINES

Hawaiian Cuisine

Virtually everything and everybody in Hawaii came from someplace else which also holds true for many of the food sources we think of as native to the island chain. The Hawaiian Islands are geologically very young. They are also among the most remote places on earth with over twenty-five hundred miles of ocean separating the islands from any major land mass. Hawaii's youth and isolation led to the evolution of a unique but nutritionally sparse flora and fauna.

The first arrivals in Hawaii are thought to have been a small dark people whose origins hail back to Southeast Asia. Archaeologists believe that these people lived off what they found which didn't go much beyond fish, birds and a few native plants. Many like to think of those earliest inhabitants as the legendary Menehune, but they, like their history, disappeared into the annals of time. It wasn't until the Polynesians sailed to Hawaii with their domestic animals and "canoe" plants that the island food resources achieved any real variety.

These ancestors of the modern Hawaiians were great mariners. A thousand years ago early groups of explorers began sailing their double-hulled voyaging canoes up from Tahiti bringing along dogs, pigs and fowl to supplement their coconuts, sweet potatoes, breadfruit, bananas, taro, yams, arrowroot and sugarcane. They also brought the Polynesian approach to cooking which includes broiling over hot coals, boiling with hot stones and roasting in an underground oven. You'll find this latter method, cooking in an imu, holding center stage at luaus today.

Ancient Hawaiians lived in ahupua'a which were land divisions reaching from the top of the mountains down adjoining ridges to the ocean. These triangular watersheds theoretically contained all the resources required to sustain distinct communities. Trees for building canoes grew up on the mountain. The uplands supported dry land crops like sweet potatoes and yams. Down along the stream beds taro was grown in wet paddies called loi. Then, beyond the coconut and breadfruit trees lay the ocean with its wealth of fish, mollusks and seaweeds.

The Hawaiian diet was simple but healthful. Fish provided the majority of the common people's protein with domestic animals and fowl reserved primarily for the ruling class and special occasions. The staple starch was poi made from the steamed and pounded corms of the taro plant. When conditions wouldn't allow for taro cultivation sweet potatoes and breadfruit were used as substitutes. Taro greens and seaweed filled the need for leafy vegetables by supplying vitamins and minerals. Finally, bananas and coconuts were important for good health.

Today these traditions continue. Modern Hawaiians usually cook like everyone else, but they make it a point to hold luaus to celebrate milestones in life. Island favorites like kalua pig, lomi lomi salmon, chicken long rice, laulau, haupia and of course poi are staples at these events. If you get the chance attend a luau and experience the original Hawaiian cuisine.

Chinese Cuisine

The Chinese have influenced the socio-economic and culinary scenes of the islands to the point that it would be difficult to imagine Hawaii without them. Beginning in the mid 1800's they were the first immigrant group recruited to work in the sugarcane fields. From those humble beginnings the Chinese went on to become the merchant class and landlords of Honolulu.

The Chinese experience in Hawaii is more than a list of menu items and real estate investments. It's become an integral part of Hawaiian history. The early Chinese immigrants came from southern China, so naturally they brought that style of cooking with them. After they arrived it didn't take them long to figure out that there wasn't much of a future working on the plantations, so as soon as their contracts expired they moved on.

These free but unemployed farmers looked around and saw opportunity. Where the Hawaiians had once raised taro and fish the Chinese saw rice paddies and duck ponds. Intermarriage provided access to idle land that soon became truck gardens and small farms. Since trading is a way of life for all Chinese, the Port of Honolulu quickly had its own Chinatown full of shops and small eateries.

Today you see the effects of this history throughout the islands. The dominant Chinese cuisine in Hawaii is Cantonese. This is the style most visitors picture when they think about eating Chinese, so the methods and menu items are quite well known. Preparations like dim sum and stir-fries are popular in the region and are standards on menus in Hawaii.

True Chinese cooking is a healthful cuisine. Chefs in China instinctively strive for balance and harmony in meal preparation. This can be accomplished by using a variety of cooking methods and ingredients. No Chinese cook would ever serve an entire deep-fried meal; rather he or she would always include vegetable dishes and offer steamed rice on the side.

To fully enjoy a Chinese meal make sure you choose a variety of dishes, levels of spiciness and cooking methods. This is banquet style dining, but can still be done at a fairly reasonable cost. Some restaurants try to make things simpler by selecting an assortment of dishes and offering them as a package, but those set menus can be a bit on the middle-of-the-road side. Make your experience an adventure and select the items yourself - just watch out for the chicken feet!

No trip to Honolulu is complete without a visit to Chinatown. Take a walk and look for the shops with the barbequed pork and smoked ducks hanging in the windows. Down off King Street you'll find markets packed with people selling vegetables you've never seen and fish so fresh they're still swimming. Finally, stop for lunch at a place where you're the only ones speaking English and there isn't a fork in sight. That's when you'll know why they call it Chinatown.

Japanese Cuisine

Like so many others the Japanese experience in Hawaii is tied to sugar. The first immigrants began arriving from Japan soon after the end of the American Civil War. At first it was a trickle, but after the Reciprocity Act Of 1876 eliminated tariffs on Hawaiian sugar the trickle turned into a torrent. That was the age of industrialized sugar, and enormous amounts of manpower were required. Today Americans of Japanese ancestry play a major role in Hawaiian society. This is reflected through Hawaii's wide variety of Japanese dining venues.

Japanese diners eat with the eyes as well as their mouths. This becomes apparent after visiting one of their restaurants. Instead of a single main entrée dominating the table the Japanese prefer variety with smaller portions served separately on various sized plates and bowls artistically arranged around the table.

The ultimate fine dining experience is the kaiseki. This is also known as royal dining or dining in courses and involves considerable ceremony along with an elegant dinner presentation. An elaborate array of special courses is served that might include items such as an exquisite appetizer, assorted sashimi and sushi, miso soup, a tempura course, a seafood dish, a small steak, pickled vegetables, steamed rice, cold noodles and dessert.

A more common choice is the teishoku or complete meal. This is the Japanese equivalent of a prix fixe dinner consisting of an appetizer, miso soup, pickled vegetables, one or two entrees, rice and perhaps dessert. Anyone interested in exploring Japanese cuisine would do well to start with a teishoku as the variety allows the diner to do some sampling and not be overwhelmed by the menu.

Within the various meal presentations you'll find a variety of preparation styles. Thanks to the spread of international dining island visitors often think of sushi and sashimi as typical Japanese food. While those are popular dishes in Japan their cuisine goes far deeper than that. Beyond the temptations of the sushi bar you will find several major styles of cooking.

First comes yakimono, which are grilled or broiled dishes. Teriyaki and yakitori are classic examples of yakimono. The knife-wielding showman in a teppanyaki steak house is also doing a form of yakimono cooking. Then you'll see agemono where meats or vegetables are fried in oil. Tempura with its light, puffy coating is probably the most recognizable form of agemono. Finally, discover nabemono where thinly sliced pieces of meat and vegetables are individually simmered in a fragrant broth using a tabletop chaffing dish. Both shabu shabu and sukiyaki are traditional nabemono dishes.

It doesn't matter if you are a culinary newcomer or an old hand, just stroll into a Japanese restaurant with confidence and after a half-bow to the hostess get ready for a truly unique and exceptional dining experience.

Portuguese Cuisine

Portuguese culinary tradition has always been the odd-man-out among Hawaiian ethnic cuisines. Where the others have Asian origins, Portuguese is European. If the Asians serve a starch it is nearly always rice. For the Portuguese starch says bread or beans. Asians love stir-fries. The Portuguese prefer stews. In spite of all this, Portuguese cooking has become a valued part of the island melting pot.

The Portuguese have always been a seafaring people. During the fourteenth and fifteenth centuries Portuguese sailors embarked on a wave of global exploration. Those adventurers brought back spices and foods that were unknown in Europe. The resulting trade routes reached around the world exposing the Portuguese to exotic places and exotic places to the Portuguese.

The first Portuguese plantation laborers arrived in Hawaii during the 1870's and were actually from the Azores and Madeira. This was a natural development as sugarcane had been part of the Madeira agricultural scene for hundreds of years. These European immigrants differed from their Asian cohorts as they intended to stay in Hawaii permanently. Their families brought hearth and home along with the entire range of Portuguese cuisine.

Hearty soups, stews and casseroles were a rather new concept in the islands but old favorites among the Portuguese. They were usually enhanced with the wide variety of spices and flavors that had come into their possession through global exploration. Portuguese sausage or linguica with its garlicky zest has gone on to become a mainstay breakfast item across the islands. In Hawaii you'll see eggs and Portuguese sausage right next to Egg McMuffins and breakfast burritos on fast food restaurant menus.

Another island favorite is Portuguese Bean Soup. If Hawaii people had to name the recipes that make their top ten list, Portuguese Bean Soup would be present every time. Somehow it doesn't seem to matter what kind of menu a restaurant normally serves or where its price range falls this local comfort food combining beans and vegetables with ham hocks and Portuguese sausage usually manages to make its way into the rotation as Soup of the Day.

Finally, there is the Portuguese tradition of baking bread. Everywhere you go in Hawaii you'll find menus offering French toast made with Portuguese sweet bread. Also known as pao doce, this local favorite has taken on another identity as Molokai Sweet Bread. Visitors to that island will see local people boarding their plane carrying loaves for those at home. Another Portuguese specialty is a sugary doughnut without a hole known as the malasada. Traditionally served as a special treat the day before Ash Wednesday, malasadas were prepared using the family's remaining butter and eggs before starting the lean times of Lent.

Korean Cuisine

Immigrants from Korea began arriving in Hawaii during the early 1900's. Like their fellows the early arrivals came to work on the plantations. Although that era is all but over, the migration continues today as Koreans seeking economic opportunity leave their homeland for Hawaii and other parts of North America.

Koreans strive for balance and harmony in all aspects of their lives. This is quite obvious at dinnertime where they look at food as a cure for physical and mental ailments as well as for sustenance. Their cuisine is low in fat and very healthful with an emphasis on grilled or broiled meats, soups and fresh vegetables. Some of the cooking methods favored by Koreans involve tableside preparation using a grill or by simmering in broth, while others require pan or deep-frying.

One item that has almost come to mean Korean is kim chee. Interestingly, both of this pickled relish's principal ingredients came from other places. The Dutch introduced cabbage to the Koreans and the chili peppers that give kim chee its fire were brought from Portugal. This zesty condiment is nearly always seen on Korean tables and adds zip to offset the mildness of rice.

Contrary to general impressions not all Korean food is highly seasoned. In fact, many of their favorite dishes could easily pass as comfort food. If people enjoy teriyaki then they'll appreciate the marinated grilled meats. Koreans are more of a beef-eating nation than most other Asian countries. It is thought that invading Mongols introduced cattle to Korea hundreds of years ago. Other protein sources common to the Korean diet include poultry and fish as well as soybean products.

For those who really must know all the details some of the ingredients used as flavoring in Korean cuisine include chrysanthemum leaves, daikon, ginger root, garlic, enokitake, shimeji and shiitake mushrooms, hot green and red peppers, green onions, mirin, miso, nori, sesame oil and seeds, pine nuts, soybean sprouts, soy sauce, tofu and wakame.

Combination meals are usually offered giving the diner a chance to experience a variety of items. These dinners begin with a variety of small dishes containing salads and pickled vegetables. Turnips, potatoes, kim chee, seaweed, garlic bulb pickles and bean sprouts among others might be offered. Soups made of oxtails, fish, chicken or vegetables, many times with the addition of beaten egg and/or dumplings are important courses in a Korean meal. Popular entrées commonly seen include bulgoki, kal bi ribs and chun. As usually found in Asian cuisines, desserts are limited to fruits and special occasion items.

Most island Korean restaurants tend to be less formal establishments where one can enjoy a healthful dinner of wonderfully prepared foods at a reasonable cost. We heartily recommend this experience to the travel adventurers whose agenda includes getting off the beaten track and rubbing elbows with the locals.

Filipino Cuisine

Filipinos constituted the last major immigrant group recruited to work Hawaii's sugarcane and pineapple plantations. Their arrival during the early to mid 1900's was a reaction to legal restrictions placed by the US government on bringing in foreign workers. The Hawaiian plantations needed cheap field labor, and as the Philippines were a US territory, it became the logical alternative.

Although at first glance one might assume that the Philippine culture would be Southeast Asian in nature that is not at all the case. Early trading visits from the east followed by three hundred years of Spanish occupation and fifty years as a US territory heavily influenced Filipino daily life. The result is truly global.

Seafaring merchants from China and Malaysia are thought to have been the first outsiders to seriously impact the culinary traditions of the Philippine archipelago. The use of egg roll wrappers in lumpia, rice, curry, coconut, coconut milk, patis, soy sauce and noodles all appear to have had their origins in eastern cuisines.

Then came the Spanish whose presence truly made an impression on the daily diet in the Philippines. Tomatoes, onion, garlic, beans, pimientos and olive oil have become everyday components in Filipino dishes. During the late 1890's America was at war with Spain and the islands came under US military control. Although Filipino people enjoy American dishes as well as their own, little of what we consider true Filipino food can be attributed to that period of history.

Today the Filipino influence on the culinary tradition in Hawaii might not be as noticeable as that of some other Asian cuisines as Main Street restaurants don't commonly serve an exclusively Filipino menu. However, that doesn't mean that visitors won't be exposed to Filipino food. Many island restaurants incorporate Filipino styles and dishes in their lineup. You just have to know where to look.

Filipino cooks like to blend all of the ingredients in a meal together rather than preparing and serving them separately. A classic example of this is adobo, which is a stew made from pork and/or chicken that have been marinated in garlic and vinegar. Another is chicken relleno, which is a roasted and boned chicken that is stuffed with a pork, onion, raisin, pimiento and hard-cooked egg stuffing.

Then come the veggies! Filipino tradition calls for the use of an extremely wide variety of vegetables. Most Western visitors won't easily identify many of them, but a walk through an Asian grocery or Chinatown will give you the picture. Of course, no meal would be complete without rice or pancit noodles on every plate.

Finally, Filipino people are fond of sweets. Look for leche flan, fruit lumpia or cascaron and you'll know you've found the dessert section of the menu. Move a little farther off the main drag and you just might find halo-halo. This refreshing island milkshake is made with ice, coconut milk and tasty fruit surprises.

Thai Cuisine

Thais were among the first immigrants to Hawaii who didn't come seeking work on the plantations. Their arrival over the last forty years was part of a movement out of Southeast Asia by those seeking greater economic opportunity. As many before them had already discovered a quick way to generate an income in a new land is to open a restaurant and introduce the neighborhood to your homeland's cuisine. Hawaii with its sizeable Asian ethnic population was a natural for these new entrepreneurs. Thai cuisine got rave reviews and quickly become a favorite.

Thai cuisine reflects an interesting history of interaction between people through out Indochina. Thanks to its central location Thailand became a crossroad for foreign travelers and exotic ideas. Immediately to the north lies China with its ancient traditions of stir-frying and the use of noodles. Among that group were Buddhists preparing vegetarian dishes. From the west came people from India making curries and Arabs cooking skewer-broiled meats. And of course don't forget the ever-present Portuguese and their tiny red hot peppers!

Chefs from Thailand have a whole arsenal of flavors at their disposal. Some of the ingredients commonly used include Thai chilies; Kaffir lime leaves, ginger, lemongrass, mint, basil, curry, peppers and the ever-present fish sauce known as nam pla. Thai food may be ordered spiced mild, medium or hot. However, since mild dishes can miss the point and hot is best reserved for the Thai's we suggest that people consider ordering medium. Then, in order to moderate the hot, spicy flavors be sure to include at least one dish that includes coconut milk and have it all served along side a steamer basket of Thai sticky rice.

Thai restaurants usually serve meals all at once rather than in courses. A number of dishes are presented giving everyone an opportunity to sample the full variety of items. Great effort is made to balance out the contrasting tastes and textures in order to promote harmony in the meal. In contrast to many Asian countries, a fork and spoon are used when dining. The fork is used for cutting and pushing food onto the spoon, while the spoon helps the diner fully appreciate the sauces.

A good rule to follow when making menu selections is to always ask, "What do the regulars order?" Naturally there are favorites like anywhere else. Starting off with the appetizer section consider the Thai Crispy Noodles or Satay Chicken. Then follow up with a Green Papaya Salad and a party-size bowl of Tom Yum Soup. Next comes the main event where dishes like Evil Prince Shrimp, Pork Pad Pet, Chicken Panang Curry and Beef with Thai Basil Sauce appear high on every list. Finally, include a platter of Pad Thai Noodles and dinner is served.

Try to visit a Thai restaurant while in you're in Hawaii. Ask for ordering advice if you need it or go it alone as you see fit. Regardless, you're a lot closer to the land the Thais call home, and that puts you in a position to discover an exciting new cuisine that truly broadens the horizons of culinary adventure.

Vietnamese Cuisine

The end of the Vietnam War signaled the beginning of a major migration out of Southeast Asia to Hawaii and North America. What began as a political exodus turned into a classic movement of people seeking a better way of life. The island state with its temperate climate and the presence of other Asian cultures became an attractive resettlement destination that draws Vietnamese immigrants to this day. Their presence has become so visible that there are those who refer to the central part of Honolulu's Chinatown historic district as Little Saigon.

While you are walking around Chinatown notice the small Vietnamese eateries that seem to be popping up on every street corner. At one time immigrants from China operated these shops. Now those people have moved on to other pursuits and the latest wave of arrivals have taken their place. Many of these places are pho shops. Pho is pronounced "fuh" and is an aromatic rice noodle soup made with a clear, rich beef stock. Fresh herbs such as Thai basil and cilantro along with bean sprouts and jalapeños are served alongside on a separate plate. The diners then flavor this popular dish to their own specifications.

Vietnamese cuisine is the result of many years of cultural blending. Like the other countries in Southeast Asia, the ebb and flow of history brought them successive waves of new multitudes and customs. The original inhabitants of Vietnam are thought to have moved down the coastline from southern China. Then newcomers from the east and west arrived looking for trade. There were occupations, first by the Chinese and then by the French. Throughout that time the people of Vietnam were learning new culinary methods and techniques.

As you peruse a Vietnamese menu you will witness those influences through the use of everything from croissants and baguettes to lemongrass and curry paste. Naturally, the Asian staple starch appears as a major item. Not only do you see rice served steamed as a side dish, but it also appears in noodles and as rice paper for wrapping. Vietnamese foods have a delicate fresh taste and are never heavy in texture or flavor. Herbs are used as greens as well as for flavor. Dishes made with curry may be ordered spiced according to your preference.

A Vietnamese meal is served family style where everyone samples each dish. Preparation is not a detailed or complicated endeavor, but rather a gathering of fresh healthful ingredients handled and cooked as little as possible. A favorite example is the banh hoi. This popular dish is made by taking grilled marinated meat slices and placing them on a moist rice paper wrapper piled with pickled daikon, carrots, bean sprouts, romaine, rice vermicelli and fresh mint leaves. This is then rolled up like a burrito and dipped into a light, flavorful sauce.

Vietnamese cuisine is the new kid on Hawaii's culinary block. Although some of the surroundings may be a little basic go on in and try this wonderful taste experience just once and you will find yourself wanting to go back for more!

Local Food

Local food is the Hawaiian Everyman's version of homegrown comfort food. Its roots go back to the plantation days when people were recruited from around the world to work the sugarcane and pineapple fields. Although they were quartered in separate camps based upon nationality, the workers gathered in small groups at lunchtime, and that is where the blending of cultures began.

The field workers' diet was pretty simple. Just about everyone had a tin of rice and some kind of meat and vegetable. A Japanese worker might bring teriyaki beef, and his Portuguese cohort would probably pack a can of sardines. Figure that the Koreans will bring along some kim chee while the Filipinos surely had adobo or lumpia. Then, in a kind of Hawaiian potluck the workers would share what they brought bringing variety to an otherwise ordinary lunch in the field.

That was the beginning of local food, but what does it look like today? When you think local food imagine something simple a plantation family would keep in their pantry. First comes the staple starch, which is nearly always rice. Then you have canned meat of which Spam, Vienna Sausages, sardines, corned beef and beef stew predominate. To add a little interest there would be a jar of mayo and a bag of macaroni with which to make a simple mac salad. Then the farmer would bring his cabbage down from upcountry and dinner would be served.

Most visitors to Hawaii experience local food at one of the lunch counters seen just about everywhere in the islands. The standard offering is commonly called plate lunch. For seven or eight dollars you get a choice of meat such as teriyaki chicken, katsu pork or mahi mahi, "two scoop" rice and a scoop of mac salad. The whole affair comes appropriately served in a Styrofoam carryout container complete with plastic table service. Bon Appetit!

If a steaming bowl of noodle soup is more your style local food accommodates as well. The staple item here is known as saimin. This dish has an interesting history. The Chinese say it has a Japanese origin and the Japanese say it came from China, so they both must be right! To make saimin first you must have a stock. In the Japanese tradition this would be a dashi which is broth made from nori flavored with bonito shavings. Since this is a little lean for many tastes the choices take off from there. Some places use chicken stock while others include pork bones in as well. Determining personal preference and figuring out who is using what is part of the adventure of exploring the local food establishments.

Don't forget the noodles that by tradition are made from wheat flour, water, and eggs. This "long rice" is complemented with a little meat and perhaps an egg as well as some Chinese cabbage to top the whole thing off. Local types will buy a teri-beef stick or two to add flavor to their bowl or as a side dish with a touch of hot mustard. We recommend beginning your saimin experience just as it arrives from the kitchen before adding a dash of hoisin or Tabasco sauce for extra zest.

Pacific Rim Cuisine

In a geographical sense Pacific Rim refers to all of the nations that border the Pacific Ocean. This area not only includes Japan, Korea, China and Southeast Asia but also takes in Australia, New Zealand and all of Polynesia as well as South, Central and North America. However, no matter how large that seems physically in a cultural sense the Pacific Rim involves even that much more.

People from diverse cultures have shared culinary traditions since the beginning of time. This interaction greatly accelerated as worldwide commercial activity, improved communications and personal travel experiences impacted the general public. During the 20th century our new awareness of different culinary practices began to change people's expectations regardless of economic status. Witness the evolving trends in the American dietary culture as we went from Italian and Chinese to Mexican and Thai. Once we began to sample we didn't want to stop.

This brings us to a better understanding of the dynamics behind the Pacific Rim movement. Watching the explosion of mass-produced ethnic convenience foods what enterprising young chef wouldn't try to capitalize on a new trend? Taking advantage of opportunity, professional chefs began using their classic training to blend ingredients from one group of countries and preparation methods from another to produce results that are on a higher level than the sum of the parts.

For instance, grilled beef tenderloin with shiitake mushrooms in a Marsala demi glace served with mashed Hawaiian taro and Okinawan sweet potatoes is a far cry from a grilled steak and baked potato. The combination utilizes Hawaiian, Chinese, French, Italian, Okinawan, Continental European and American foods and methods to elevate the diner's experience. The chef's formal training and experience in blending flavors led to the resulting balanced and pleasing entree.

In the Hawaiian Islands travelers sometimes wonder if they are being offered Pacific Rim or Hawaii Regional Cuisine. Hawaii Regional Cuisine showcases locally produced fish, meats, fruits and vegetables combined with local ethnic styles and classic cooking techniques to create an upscale, contemporary version of Hawaiian "local food". Pacific Rim Cuisine draws upon a much broader area when sourcing ingredients and cooking methods while producing an innovative fusion of cuisines from all around the Pacific Rim.

A visit to a Pacific Rim restaurant is like a trip to a foodie theme park. As you read the menu try and picture the tastes and ingredients the chef is combining before you make your selection. Not all the world's flavors and textures are to everyone's liking. By thinking about what you really enjoy and then following your own lead you will be much better prepared to select those dishes most likely to please so you can experience a truly enjoyable dining experience.

Hawaii Regional Cuisine

There was a time when fine dining in Hawaii was a less than stellar experience. Much of what appeared on the restaurant menus had to be shipped in over long distances. Anything that could be shipped frozen and whatever couldn't arrived tired. Then, in order to try and please the visitors, the local chefs tried to prepare classic cuisine under less than ideal circumstances. As you can imagine, cooking Continental out of a can didn't work very well.

Along came the late 1980's and a group of young chefs decided that something had to be done to improve the situation. They began talking with local farmers, fishermen and ranchers about the types of products needed to raise the level of their culinary offerings. Then, in order to create new and exciting dishes these chefs began merging local cultural influences with their newfound sources of supply, and Hawaii Regional Cuisine was on its way to being born

In the original group there were twelve chefs who banded together and formally created the Hawaii Regional Cuisine movement. Those twelve were: Sam Choy, Roger Dikon, Mark Ellman, Bev Gannon, Jean Marie Josselin, George (Mavro) Mavrothalassitis, Peter Merriman, Amy Ferguson Ota, Philippe Padovani, Alan Wong and Roy Yamaguchi. It was their goal to combine fresh island products with local ethnic cooking styles and classic techniques to create a contemporary upscale regional cuisine exclusive to Hawaii.

Hawaii Regional Cuisine is a fusion of elements from both eastern and western cultures. Much of the inspiration then comes from the simple beginnings of the plantation camps and what islanders call "local food". Add that to an innovative group of classically trained chefs and the freshest of local products and you get truly unique preparations unlike anything you've ever experienced.

There are an amazing variety of offerings on a Hawaii Regional Cuisine menu. Naturally, fresh island fish like opakapaka and mahi-mahi appear regularly, but so do local aquaculture products like Kahuku prawns and Keahole lobster. Look for the Asian preparations and Polynesian sauces that take these specialties one-step beyond. Then to complement the seafood dishes you might find innovative items like pineapple chicken or macadamia crusted lamb rounding things out.

While you are traveling in the islands keep an eye out for restaurants operated by any of the twelve original Hawaii Regional Cuisine chefs. They will surely provide you with a memorable evening of dining enjoyment. There's also a new group of young up and coming chefs who are doing wonderful work in Hawaii. They call themselves the Hawaiian Island Chefs and include Steve Ariel, Chai Chaowasaree, Hiroshi Fukui, Teri Gannon, George Gomes, Wayne Hirabayashi, D. K. Kodama, Lance Kosaka, Jacqueline Lau, Douglas Lum, James McDonald, Mark Okumura, Russell Siu, Goren Streng and Corey Waite. Look for them as you choose your next dining spot. They're the new wave and they're here today.

Kauai

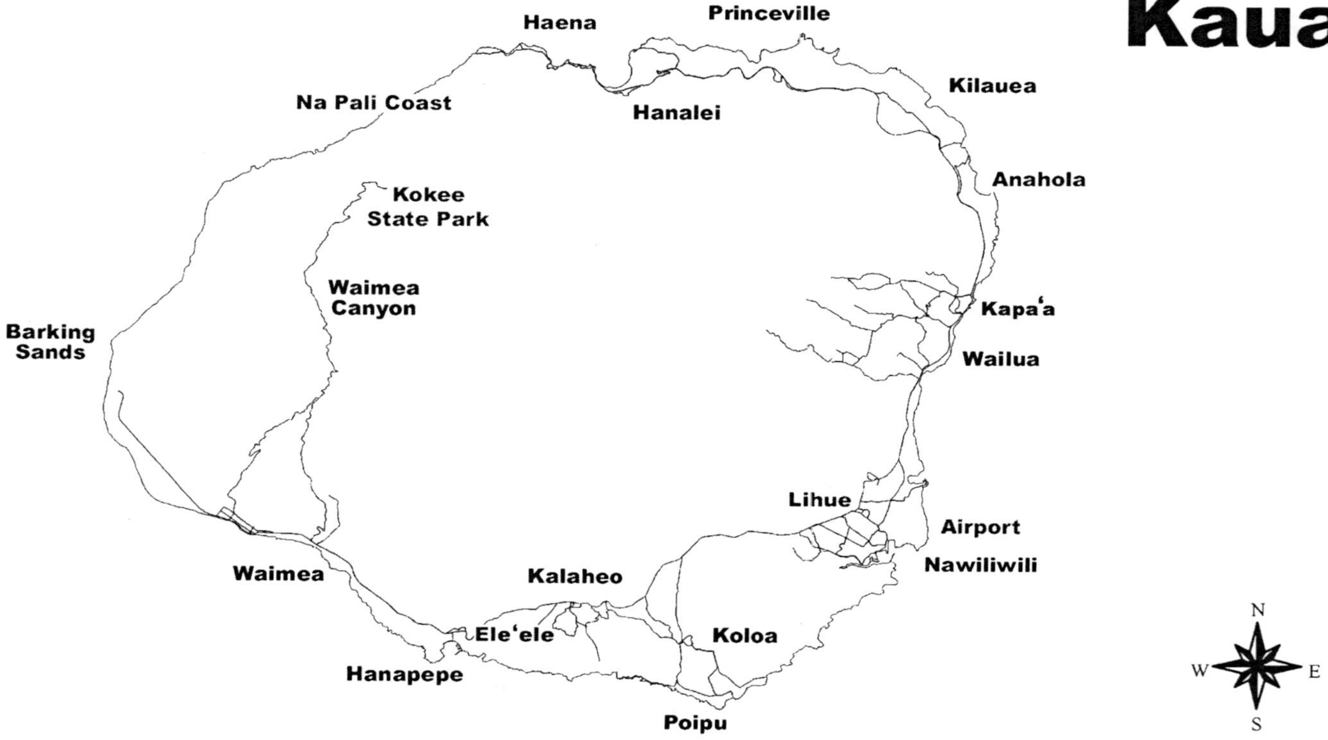

Haena
Princeville
Na Pali Coast
Hanalei
Kilauea
Anahola
Kokee
State Park
Waimea
Canyon
Kapa'a
Barking
Sands
Wailua
Lihue
Airport
Nawiliwili
Waimea
Kalaheo
Ele'ele
Koloa
Hanapepe
Poipu

N
W
E
S

KAUAI
DINING

Kauai Dining

North Shore

Bar Acuda ✓✓✓
Hanalei Center
5-5161 Kuhio Hwy (Hwy 56)
Hanalei, HI 96714
808-826-7081
www.restaurantbaracuda.com
Hours: D 6:00 PM-9:30 PM XMo
Cards: DIS MC V
Dress: Resort Casual
Style: Tapas/Light Bites/Dinner/Wine Bar $$

Menu Sampler: Small Plates Too

Breakfast/Lunch:
N/A
Dinner:
Tapas: Mediterranean olives with citrus and fennel $6, Roasted fingerling potatoes with pepita seed and apple aioli $9, Endive salad apple, candied walnuts and Stilton blue cheese $12, Bruschetta whole roasted tomatoes, leeks and balsamic $8.5, House cured chorizo sausage with grilled apple $9, Ahi carpaccio of thinly sliced tuna with chili, lime and cilantro $12,Cacalao of warm salt cod with garlic, potatoes, cream and crostini $10, Banderillas of grilled flank steak skewers with honey and chipotle chili oil $12, Giant "day boat" sea scallop with truffled mashed potatoes $12, Pizzetta with prosciutto, mozzarella and arugula $15, Marshall farm honeycomb with Humboldt fog goat cheese, mizuna greens and apples $12, Roasted pork rack chop with roasted apples, onion rings and Marsala wine reduction sauce $27, Hawaiian mahi-mahi $28
Desserts: Chocolate pot de crème $7.5, Biscotti and cookie plate $8, Coconut ice cream with gingered pineapple $9, Affogato vanilla ice cream and shot of espresso $6, Molten Chocolate cake with almond ice cream $9
Coffee & Tea: French Roast $2.5, Espresso $3.5, Cappuccino $3.5
Adult Beverages: Beer/Wine Cellar/Cocktails - Corkage Fee $15

Impressions: Intimate Hideaway

Those looking for the tapas/wine bar scene on the north shore of Kauai will find an excellent example at Bar Acuda. Early starters can arrive at five to watch the chef go over the day's specialties with the staff. After all, the central preparation area is right behind the bar. Then, at six you can indulge your culinary fantasies by ordering whatever daily special catches your imagination. The selections will follow Mediterranean tradition down to including imported ingredients. Finally, you match your small plates with appropriate beverage pairings and bon appetit!

h Shore

se Restaurant ✓✓✓

5022 Lawai Road
Koloa, HI 96756
808-742-1424
www.the-beach-house.com
Hours: D 5:30 PM-10:00 PM
Cards: AE DC MC V
Dress: Resort Casual
Style: Pacific Rim $$$

Must make a reservation!

Menu Sampler: Kids Menu Too

Breakfast/Lunch:
N/A

Dinner:
Appetizers: Togarashi Fried Calamari with guava cocktail sauce 10, Ahi Taster ahi sashimi, ahi tostadas, ahi spring roll 18, Macadamia Nut Crab Cakes with papaya black bean salsa, coconut red curry and ginger beurre blanc 12
Soup & Salad: Omao Baby Lettuce, roasted sesame orange vinaigrette 7, Seafood Corn Chowder with crab, fresh fish, chives, sherry 8, Blackened Ahi Caesar with romaine lettuce, feta & parmesan cheese and herb crouton 13
Entrées: Chinese Style Roasted Duck, lemon orange Grand Marnier demi, porcini risotto cake, pickled vegetables, pesto 26, Filet Mignon, peppered sweet onion, au gratin potato, red wine demi-glace 30, Wasabi Crusted Snapper, lilikoi lemon grass beurre blanc 30, Mint Coriander Marinated Lamb Rack with goat cheese, roasted garlic crust and mint au jus 34, Oven Roasted Breast of Chicken stuffed with wild mushrooms and gorgonzola, herbed polenta cake, port wine demi 26, Seafood & Penne Pasta in saffron cream, oyster mushrooms 26
Desserts: Hawaiian Chocolate Haupia Cake 10, Bananas Foster, mac nuts 9, Molten Chocolate Desire 10 (allow 20 minutes for preparation)
Adult Beverages: Beer/Wine Cellar/Cocktails – Corkage Fee 25

Impressions: Ultra Waterfront

The Beach House owns one of the most dramatic settings you'll find in Hawaii. Outside, there's the Pacific Ocean splashing up on the rocks. Inside, diners find fine Pacific Rim cuisine served in a casual yet upscale atmosphere. Their menu has been expanded recently and offers a nice variety of enticing selections. This special dining spot is always busy so make reservations. Valet parking is almost a must as there is no lot on the premises and street parking is very limited in the surrounding area. Pupu and cocktail service begins at 5 PM so stop in early and secure your seat for the fabulous sunset viewing. We prefer the lounge early on.

South Shore

Brennecke's Beach Broiler ✓✓✓

2100 Hoone Road
Koloa, HI 96756
808-742-7588
www.brenneckes.com

Hours: L 11:00 AM-4:00 PM
D 4:00 PM-9:30 PM
Cards: AE DC DIS MC V
Dress: Casual
Style: Island/Eclectic $$$

Menu Sampler:

Kids Menu Too

Breakfast:
N/A

Lunch:
Pupus: Ceviche 'n Chips 9.50, Seared Ahi 13.50, Nachos w/black beans & peppers 11.50, Shrimp Cocktail 11.50, Sashimi of Ahi w/soy & mustard 12.95
Soups, Salads, Sandwiches: Fresh Hawaiian Ahi Sandwich 13.95, Prime Rib Sandwich 14.95, NE Style Clam Chowder 3.95/5.95, Ahi Caesar Salad 14.95, Soup, Salad Bar, Bread Combo 13.50, Chicken Caesar Salad 14.50, BBQ Kalua Pork Sandwich, guava plum BBQ Sauce, fries 13.95, Fresh Fish Tacos (2) 14.95

Dinner:
Pupus: Shrimp Stuffed Mushrooms 12.95, Kama'aina Pupu Platter 15.95, Spicy Black Mussels in a white wine broth 9.95, Crispy Calamari with sauce 8.95
Entrées: All entrées are served with choice of salad bar or chowder, sautéed vegetables, steamed rice or herb pasta and dinner roll. Fresh Island Fish kiawe broiled or sautéed with lemon caper sauce 27.50, Ginger Sesame Crusted Opah 28.50, Cajun Spiced Grilled Mahi Mahi 28.50, Brennecke's Special Scampi over pasta 27.95, Spicy Lemongrass Shrimp Stir Fry 26.50, Baby Back Pork BBQ Ribs 25.95, Prime Rib 21.50/28.95, New York Steak with sautéed mushrooms 26.95, Cioppino of shrimp, fresh fish, mussels & crab in a hearty vegetable broth 27.50, Chicken Alfredo 21.50, Fresh Vegetables & Tofu over rice 19.95
Adult Beverages: Beer/Wine/Cocktails – Corkage Fee 15.00

Impressions:

Casual Beachcomber

First time visitors to Brennecke's might get the impression that they're in South Florida instead of Hawaii. The flat roofed two story building would probably be as much at home on Key Largo as in Poipu Beach. The same goes for the menu where contemporary island preparations are the specialty of the house. Presume great fish choices and interesting seafood spins at this casual beachfront walkup.

West Side

Brick Oven Pizza ✓✓

2-2555 Kaumualii Hwy (Hwy 50)
Kalaheo, HI 96741
808-332-8561
Web: None
Hours: LD 11:00 AM-10:00 PM XMo
Cards: MC V
Dress: Casual
Style: Italian/Family Style $

Menu Sampler:

Breakfast:
N/A
Lunch/Dinner:
Pizza: Hearth Baked Pizzas made of whole wheat or white crust brushed with garlic butter $11.00 - $33.45 in 10"/12"/15" sizes, Pizza Bread (one slice) $3.10 w/traditional ingredients such as Italian sausage (they make their own), salami, pepperoni, black olives, mushrooms, anchovies or Seafood Style Pizza Bread w/bay shrimp, cheddar cheese, green onions, pizza sauce or garlic butter $3.60
Sandwiches: Hot Super Sandwich of smoked ham, salami, pepperoni, cheese, mustard, lettuce, tomatoes, onions $7.30, Italian Sausage Sandwich of Italian sausage, pizza sauce, cheese, lettuce, tomatoes, white onions $7.65, Garlic Bread $.80/slice, with cheese $1.35/slice, Roast Beef Sandwich au jus, white onion $7.65, Open Face Sandwich of smoked ham, tomato, provolone cheese $7.75, Chicken Sandwich with Italian seasonings, mayo, onion $7.30
Salads: Veggie Salad of greens, zucchini, mushrooms, bell pepper, black olives, onions, mozzarella and cheddar cheese in small $4.15 or large $6.25
Desserts: Aloha Pie $3.00, Double Chocolate Cake $3.30, Cheese Cake $3.00
Adult Beverages: Beer/Wine

Impressions: Family Pizzeria

The village of Kalaheo is just a short distance from Koloa and Poipu Beach. As you enter town you'll see Brick Oven Pizza mauka of the highway. Here you'll find one of the best pizzas on Kauai. The garlic butter-brushed crust is excellent and comes with a wide variety of traditional toppings. Vegetarians will like the sauce as it's made without meat or poultry stock. Everybody will like the 100% real mozzarella cheese! Brick Oven Pizza is family owned and has been serving high quality food at reasonable prices since 1970. In keeping with Italian family dining tradition, beer and wine are available. Customers can dine in or carry out.

North Shore

CJ's Steak & Seafood ✓✓✓

Princeville Center
5-4280 Kuhio Hwy (Hwy 56)
Princeville, HI 96722
808-826-6211
Web: None
Hours: L 11:30 AM-2:30 PM Mo-Fr
D 6:00 PM-9:30 PM
Cards: AE DC DIS JCB MC
Dress: Casual
Style: Steak & Seafood/Salad Bar $$$

Menu Sampler: Kids Menu Too

Breakfast:
N/A
Lunch:
Salads: Caesar Salad with Blackened Fillet of Ono 10.50, Crab Louie 13.50
Sandwiches: All include fries, tossed greens or onion rings. CJ's Burger 1/3 # 8.25, CJ's Prime Rib Sandwich 10.75, Tuna or Turkey Melt 9.75, BLT 8.25
Dinner:
Pupus: Thai Spring Rolls with CJ's special sauces 6.50, Steamed Artichokes 6.75, Mushrooms Sauté in wine and butter, lightly seasoned 7.25, Sashimi 8.95
Entrées: Salad Bar 10.50. All dinners include the salad bar with vegetables, fruits, hot rolls and your choice of rice pilaf or steamed white rice. Catch of the Day Broiled, Baked, Sautéed or Cajun 26.95, CJ's Shrimp Dinners sautéed in butter, white wine, lemon juice, herbs; or battered deep fried macadamia nut coconut with sauces; or teriyaki style broiled 29.95, Prime Filet of Tenderloin 34.95, Prime Rib 29.95/26.95/23.95, Barbequed Baby Back Pork Ribs 26.25, New Zealand Rack of Lamb 29.95, Teriyaki Chicken Breasts broiled 23.25
Seniors (over 60) and Children (under 12): Includes rice and salad bar. Teriyaki Chicken Breast 14.50, Shrimp Hanalei 16.95, Hamburger Patty 10.95
Adult Beverages: Beer/Wine/Cocktails – Corkage Fee 5.00 L / 10.00 D

Impressions: Island Standard

Those who've been knocking around Kauai for some time might remember CJ's when they operated under the Chuck's Steak House moniker. Twenty-five years later the formula remains the same. This is a traditional steak & seafooder of the old school complete with wood décor and salad bar. Dinner is the primary event with lunch being served only on weekdays. The menu includes the usual butcher block and fish monger favorites with a creative nod toward contemporary tastes.

Café Portofino ✓✓✓
Kauai Marriott Resort
3610 Rice Street
Nawiliwili, HI 96766
808-245-2121
www.cafeportofino.com
Hours: D 5:00 PM-9:30 PM
Cards: AE DC DIS MC V
Dress: Resort Casual
Style: Classic Italian $$$

Menu Sampler: Small Plates Too

Breakfast/Lunch:
N/A
Dinner:
Appetizers: Steamed Clams, Mixed Deep Ocean Fish, Sautéed Scallops, Fried Calamari, Escargot, Antipasto Platter, Mozzarella Caprese, Ahi Carpaccio
Soups: Minestrone, Cappelletti in Broth, Bouillabaisse, Gaspacio served cold
Salads: Mixed Garden Greens or Caesar Salad served with house dressings
Pasta: Spaghetti Marinara, Fettuccini Alfredo, Linguine Pesto, Penne Broccoli & Spinach, Linguine Carbonara, Cheese Ravioli, Chicken Cannelloni, Lasagna
Entrées: Fresh Island Fish w/Choice of Preparations, Dover Sole, Lobster Tail, Scallops, Scampi, New York Strip, Rib Eye, Filet Mignon, Pork T-Bone, Rack of Lamb, Veal or Chicken Piccata, Marsala, or Porcini, Osso Buco, Surf & Turf
Desserts: Profiteroles, Tiramisu, Panna Cotta, Gelatos, Sorbets, Carmel Custard
Adult Beverages: Beer/Wine Cellar/Cocktails – Corkage Fee

Impressions: Upscale Italian

This romantic white linen and black tie restaurant recently relocated to new digs next to Duke's Kauai on Kalapaki Beach. The specialty of the house is Northern Italian cuisine, and you'll have to look hard to find better. Everything is cooked to perfection with fresh herbs and fine sauces used throughout. Black tie service is elegant but unobtrusive. Whether you prefer a table set inside or out, you'll be treated to a gracious continental experience with tropical flair. Café Portofino is one of our personal favorite dining experiences and comes highly recommended.

South Shore

Casablanca at Kiahuna ✓✓✓

Kiahuna Tennis Club
2290 Poipu Road
Koloa, HI 96756
808-742-2929
Web: None
Hours: L 11:00 AM-3:00 PM
D 5:30 PM-9:00 PM
Cards: DIS MC V
Dress: Resort Casual
Style: Mediterranean $$$

Menu Sampler:

Kids Menu Too

Breakfast:
N/A
Lunch:
Salads: Spinach with a roasted garlic-Dijon vinaigrette, pancetta, pine nuts $10
Entrées: Panini of mozzarella, prosciutto, onions or grilled vegetables $8, Casa Pita Plate with grilled lamb, mint yogurt dressing, spicy harissa $12, Casablanca PMT with grilled Prosciutto, fresh mozzarella and tomato on ciabatta $9
Dinner:
Entrées: Crispy Seared Duck Breast flavored with a balsamic glaze of capers and garlic served with mashed root vegetables $19, Ribeye Steak dry-rubbed with sugar & salt, seasoned with porcini mushroom powder, red pepper flakes and garlic, drizzled with a balsamic vinegar reduction, roasted potatoes $26, Spanish seafood stew of lobster, shrimp, scallops, calamari and mussels in a savory broth $28, Chicken Toscano, fettuccini with a light brandy sauce $18
Tapas: Eggplant Caponata Agrodolce with raisins, olives, capers and pine nuts $5, Moroccan B'Steeya Crepe, chicken, cinnamon, saffron and almonds $7, Hummus with lemon, cumin and garlic served with pita $6, Gambas Al Ajillo of sizzling shrimp with garlic and crushed pepper flakes in olive oil & bread $12
Adult Beverages: Beer/Wine/Cocktails – Corkage Fee $10

Impressions:

Flavor Slam

Centered in the Kiahuna resort's pool and tennis club complex there's a jewel of a restaurant serving the exciting tastes of the Mediterranean. Throughout the day visitors to Casablanca can enjoy a step away from the ordinary. This is al fresco dining where bold tastes rule and the timid need not apply. Happy hour habitués can graze one of the best tapas menus in Hawaii. If there's time sample another!

South Shore

Casa di Amici ✓✓

2301 Nalo Road
Koloa, HI 96756
808-742-1555
Web: None
Hours: D 6:00 PM-8:30 PM
Cards: DC MC V
Dress: Resort Casual
Style: Italian/Seafood/Pacific Rim $$$

Menu Sampler: Kids Menu Too

Breakfast/Lunch:
N/A
Dinner:
Pupus: Gnocchi Quatro Formaggio with four cheese filling with a tomato-sage-pancetta sauce gratineed with Grana Padano Parmesan $15, Calamari Fritte breaded in Panko Flakes in a piccatta sauce $15, Chesapeake Bay style crab cakes with a passion fruit lobster sauce $15, Chili Verde Risotto with tortilla $15
Salades: Insalata Di Pomodoro of sliced tomatoes, sweet red onions, fresh mozzarella, olive tapenade and fresh basil with a raspberry vinaigrette $8, Asian Salade Mesciun with goat cheese, mac nuts and sesame-ginger vinaigrette $8
Pasta: Fettucine Alfredo $17, Scampi Di Amici garlic linguine $25, Poached Salmon and Black Tiger Pawns with lobster-cognac sauce on linguine $19
Entrées: Tournedos Rossini sautéed medallions of filet finished in a Madeira-shallot sauce, served with an Asian spiced pate, fluted mushroom caps atop garlic croutons $26, Veal Piccatta of sautéed veal scaloppini finished in a chardonnay lemon-caper sauce $20/$25, Classic Duck Confit $20/25, Grilled Ahi with red miso-ginger sauce light and beluga black lentils $20/$25, Japanese Mahogany Glazed Salmon and Grilled Black Tiger Prawns served on black frijoles chonitos $25, Braised Lamb Shank in demi glace and cabernet $25, Filet Mignon Campania served in a light and dark peppercorn sauce $25
Adult Beverages: Beer/Wine/Cocktails – Corkage Fee $15

Impressions: Neighborhood Bistro

This engaging dining spot is located in a residential neighborhood behind Poipu Beach. Casa di Amici features upscale Italian fare with Pacific Rim influence on their ambitious, well-executed menu. The combination adds an exotic spin when applied to some of the preparations. Others are left true to their origins allowing diners to suit their own preference. Reservations are a must at this romantic little restaurant. Parking in the lot is limited and impossible on the street so dine early.

West Side

Da Imu Hut Café ✓✓

1-3959 Kaumualii Hwy (Hwy 50)
Hanapepe, HI 96716
808-335-0200
Web: None
Hours: L 10:00 AM-1:30 PM Mo-Fr
L 10:00 AM-1:00 PM Sa
D 5:00 PM-8:00 PM Mo-Fr
Cards: None
Dress: Casual
Style: Island/Local $

Menu Sampler: Small Plates Too

Breakfast:
N/A
Lunch/Dinner:
Hawaiian Plate: with Kalua Pork or Pork Laulau served with lomilomi salmon, poi, rice and potato mac salad $7.75
Local Style Plates: served with two scoops rice and potato mac salad, Imu Hut Fried Chicken $6.85, Imu Hut Teri-Fried Chicken $6.95, Hamburga Steak $6.25, Teri Beef $7.50. All mini-plates $4.85 (smaller portions), Mini Teri-Beef $5.70, Fried Saimin Plate (noodles pan fried with bacon, green onions & fish cake) $6.50, Loco Moco with one hamburger patty, two scoops rice, two over easy eggs & brown gravy $5.75, Combo Plates $7.25 with any two choices of Imu Hut Fried Chicken, Imu Hut Teri-Fried Chicken, Teri-Beef, Hamburga Steak or Fried Saimin with two scoop rice & potato mac salad. All mini-combo plates (smaller portion) $5.85, Alii Saimin, hot shrimp base broth $5.50/$6.50/$7.50
Sandwiches: served with lettuce and tomato, Hamburga $3.75, Teriburga $4.00, Cheeseburga $4.25, Bacon Cheeseburga $4.50, Shoestring Fries $2.00
Adult Beverages: N/A

Impressions: Island Kine

Down Hanapepe way people still move at the slower pace of Old Hawaii. In fact it took ten years for Da Imu Hut to find its way out to the main highway from its original location inside the village. Now the rest of us can find this simple island treasure that was formerly known only to the local crowd. The news here is high quality island food that's served at extremely reasonable prices. The meat is well trimmed, and the side dishes come across as made-to-order. Everything we tried clicked, but we really like the Hawaiian Plate and the Fried Chicken. Picnic food and carry outs are big here. This makes a great stop when you're going west side.

Lihue

Dani's Restaurant ✓
4201 Rice Street
Lihue, HI 96766
808-245-4991
Web: None
Hours: BL 5:00 AM-1:00 PM XSu
Cards: MC V
Dress: Casual
Style: American/Island/Local $

Menu Sampler:

Breakfast:
Breakfast Steak with two eggs, Hamburger Steak with two eggs and brown gravy, Two Eggs with choice of bacon, links, Spam, Vienna or Portuguese sausage, Cheese Omelet, Ham & Cheese Omelet, Scafood Omelet, Dani's Special Omelet, Mushroom Omelet, all served with your choice of rice, buttered toast, or hash browns and Kona blend coffee or hot tea
Specials: Bacon (3) Eggs (2) Hot Cakes (3), Pineapple, Papaya or Banana Hot Cakes (3), Short Stack (2), Golden Brown Waffle, Sweet Bread French Toast (2)
Lunch:
Breakfast & Lunch Specialties: Lau Lau and Lomi Salmon with rice or poi, Kalua Pig and Lomi Salmon with rice or poi, Beef or Tripe Stew with rice or poi
Entrées: Fried Pork Chops, Hamburger Steak, Teriyaki Beef or Chicken, Cutlet with choice of meat and brown gravy, Crisp Fried Chicken, Breaded Mahi Mahi, Seafood Platter, Fried Shrimp, Oysters or Scallops all served with rice and salad
Sandwiches: Hamburger, Cheeseburger, Deluxe Burgers, Ham & Cheese, Tuna Salad, Ham and Egg, Deviled Egg, Bacon-Lettuce-Tomato, Grilled Cheese
Salads: Stuffed Tomato, Chef's Salad, Mac and Potato Salad, Tossed Greens
Adult Beverages: N/A
Dinner:
N/A

Impressions: Local Cafe

A visit to Dani's is a great introduction to family dining Lihue style. Everything about this place says small town café. The day begins at 5AM when the regulars file in for breakfast. Then the family crowd takes over and things get a tad busy. Meanwhile, business types come-and-go giving one the impression that this is as much a community center as a restaurant. Everyone is here to enjoy what island people call local food. The menu items might come across as simple, but they're well prepared and affordable. Budget types and light appetites will do well here.

South Shore

Dondero's ✓✓✓
Grand Hyatt Kauai Resort & Spa
1571 Poipu Road
Koloa, HI 96756
808-742-6260
www.kauai.hyatt.com
Hours: D 6:00 PM-10:00 PM
Cards: AE DC DIS JCB MC V
Dress: Resort Casual
Style: Italian $$$$

Menu Sampler:

Kids Menu Too

Breakfast/Lunch:
N/A
Dinner:
Insalate: Caesar Salad $10.50, Mixed Green Salad with Extra Virgin Olive Oil and Balsamic Vinegar $9.50, Burrata Cheese & Kamuela Tomatoes $17.00
Antipasti: Carpaccio with truffle oil $15.50, Fried Calamari in a spicy pepper aioli $12.50, Fish & Octopus Carpaccio with heirloom tomato salad $18.00
Pasta: Black Ink Lasagna with scallops, shrimp, lobster, crab in tomato and béchamel $34.00, Pappardelle with pheasant and morel mushroom sauce $28.00
Entrées: Rack of Lamb with gorgonzola and cauliflower soufflé in a balsamic sauce $42.00, Beef Filet topped with cured Foie Gras and sautéed Pioppini Mushrooms $38.50, Pan Roasted Sea Bass with fava beans, roasted shallots, baby zucchini, olives and fresh tomato concasse and caper dressing $36.00, Veal Rib Eye with pink peppercorn and artichoke sauce $40.00, Olive Crusted Ahi Tuna served with Caponata $34.00, Sautéed Prawns and large Scallops on peperonata and celery root salsa $38.00, Ossobuco alla Milanese $39.00
Desserts: Tiramisu $8.00, Amaretto Cheesecake with fresh berry sauce $8.50
Adult Beverages: Beer/Wine Cellar/Cocktails – Corkage Fee Varies

Impressions:

Fine Italian

Dondero's offers a dining experience that's completely in step with its location in Poipu's benchmark resort. Just as The Hyatt Kauai Resort & Spa focuses on indulging oneself their signature Italian restaurant can always be counted on for an evening of superb fine dining. The perfect ending to a busy day begins when you are escorted into the elegantly appointed room or out onto the terrace. Then things move on to choices from an extensive wine list before choosing from the Epicurean level Northern Italian menu. After dinner remain at your table for an amaretto concoction or move on to Stevenson's for conversation and live music.

Kauai Dining

North Shore

Duane's Ono-Char Burger ✓✓
4-4350 Kuhio Hwy (Hwy 56)
Anahola, HI 96703
808-822-9181
Web: None
Hours: LD 10:00 AM-6:00 PM XSu
LD 11:00 AM-6:00 PM Su
Cards: MC V
Dress: Casual
Style: American $

Menu Sampler:

Kids Menu Too

Breakfast:
N/A
Lunch/Dinner:
Burgers: Ono (ono means delicious) Burger with lettuce and tomato, regular $4.15, Ono Cheeseburger $4.65, Old Fashioned Burger with cheddar, onion, sprouts, Kaiser roll $5.20, Teriyaki Burger (biggest seller)$4.70, BBQ Burger $4.70, Blue Cheese Burger $4.90, Avocado Burger $6.45, Local Boy Burger, teriyaki with cheddar and grilled pineapple $5.90, Duane's Special $6.45
Sandwiches: Grilled Chicken $5.25, Patty Melt $4.95, Grilled Cheese $3.00, Combo (vegetarian) $5.25, Fish $5.75, Avocado $5.75, Tuna/Avocado $7.00
Specialties: Deep Fried Shrimp & Fries $7.75, Fish & Chips Sm. (1 pc) $3.65, Med. (2 pcs) $5.00, Lrg. (3 pcs) $6.50, Chicken & Chips (5 pcs) $7.25
Side Orders & Beverages: French Fries $1.20/$2.05, Onion Rings $2.50, Corn Dog $2.00, Ono's Tossed Green Salad $3.50, Papaya, Banana, Pineapple Juice & Crushed Ice $2.25/$2.50, Ice Cream Floats & Freezes $3.25
Adult Beverages: BYOB

Impressions:

Burger Stand

Duane's doesn't serve haute cuisine. This is a hamburger stand; nothing more, nothing less. Customers walk up to the window, place their orders, and wait to be called. As the name implies the patties are flame-grilled. They aren't overly large, but they come with a wild variety of toppings packed into a quality bun. Everything is served in paper wrappings ready to carry out or bring over to the nearby picnic tables for a quick lunch. Those new to Duane's should note that there are no restroom facilities on site. Wise parents might want to plan ahead.

Lihue

Duke's Kauai ✓✓

Kauai Marriott Resort & Beach Club
3610 Rice Street
Lihue, HI 96766
808-246-9599
www.dukeskauai.com
Hours: L 11:00 AM-11:00 PM
D 5:00 PM-10:00 PM
Cards: AE DC DIS MC V
Dress: Resort Casual
Style: American/Seafood $$

Menu Sampler:

Kids Menu Too

Breakfast:
N/A

Lunch @ Barefoot Bar:
Duke's Nachos 8.95, Mango BBQ Baby Back Ribs 12.95, Teriyaki Burger 8.95, Cashew Chicken Stir Fry 11.95, Fish Tacos (2) 12.95, Caesar Salad with Grilled Chicken 10.95, with Mahi Mahi 12.95, Pepperoni Pizza 8.95, Hula Pie 6.95

Dinner:
Each selection includes the house salad bar serving Duke's tossed salad, freshly baked muffins and sourdough bread. Fresh island fish prepared in several ways such as baked in a garlic, lemon and sweet basil glaze, sautéed mac nut and herb crusted with lemon caper butter, grilled island style with pineapple chutney and lemon beurre blanc, lime and chili roasted tomato, onion and cilantro crusted or seared ahi with seven spices and papaya mustard sauce Market, Shrimp Scampi or Macadamia Nut Pesto Linguine 19.95, Steak and Lobster Market, Chinese Style Beef Short Ribs 21.95, Ribeye Peppersteak 28.95, Prime Rib 26.95, Huli Huli Chicken and Baby Back Pork Ribs 19.95, Kushiyaki brochette 18.95

Adult Beverages: Beer/Wine/Cocktails – Corkage Fee 10.00

Impressions:

(See "Ultimate Kauai") South Seas

Duke's Kauai is located down Kalapaki Beach from the Kauai Marriott Resort. This large, open-air restaurant is built around an indoor tropical landscape that would look at home on a Hollywood sound stage. Even the table tops are made from native woods and have been labeled with their island names. The terraced dining room and spacious Barefoot Bar offer patrons a front seat on Nawiliwili Bay. Dinner is the main event at Duke's with the mid-priced steak and seafood menu served in generous portions. A lite menu is available throughout the day for those looking for a late lunch, a little shade or just coming in off the beach.

Lihue

Garden Island Barbecue and Chinese Restaurant ✓

4252 Rice Street
Lihue, HI 96766
808-245-8868
Web: None
Hours: LD 10:00 AM-9:00 PM XSu
Cards: None
Dress: Casual
Style: Chinese $

Menu Sampler:

Kids Menu Too

Breakfast:
N/A
Lunch/Dinner:
Appetizer: Deep Fried Won Ton (8 pieces) $4.25, Pork Char Siu $6.50, Deep Fried Gau Gee (7 pieces) $4.25, Deep Fried Spring Rolls (4 pieces) $4.95
Soup: Wor Won Ton Mein $6.95, Long Rice Egg Drop Soup $6.95, Minced Chicken with Cream Corn Soup $6.95, Scallop Soup $8.95, Abalone Soup $9.95
Entrées: Chicken with Black Mushrooms $6.95, Roast Duck with Pineapple $7.95, Beef or Pork with Choi Sum $6.95, Beef or Pork with Bitter Melon $6.95, Roast Pork w/Un Choi or Mixed Vegetables $7.95, Abalone with Black Mushrooms $9.95, Tenderloin Steak w/Black Pepper $8.95, Ma Po Tofu $6.95
Vegetarian: Choi Sum with Oyster Sauce or Bittermelon & Black Bean Sauce $6.95, Broccoli with Garlic $6.95, Eggplant with Tofu or Choi Sum $6.95
Chow Mein: Chicken or Pork Fried Noodle $6.95, Seafood Chow Mein $7.95
Plate Lunch: Includes 2 scoops of rice and 1 scoop of macaroni salad or kim chee. BBQ Chicken & Chicken Katsu $6.50, Sweet and Sour Spare Ribs & Fried Shrimp $6.50, Char Siu & Garlic Shrimp $6.50, Loco Moco $6.50
Sandwiches: Hamburger $1.50, Teri Beef $2.75, Shrimp Burger $2.75
Side Orders: Saimin $3.50/$4.00/$4.50, Teri Beef Saimin $4.00/$4.50/$5.50
Adult Beverages: BYOB

Impressions:

Kauai Ethnic

Those of us with time and grade probably remember when going out for Chinese meant extensive menus with bargain prices. Good traditions still apply at Garden Island Barbecue. This is the kind of place where old tastes rule and exotic dishes need not apply. Local guests are catered to with a wide selection of plate lunches and sandwiches. Everything is well prepared using flavorful sauces that enhance but don't dominate. Large portion sizes encourage family dining so bring friends or a big appetite. There's extra parking behind the restaurant if the curbs are full.

Kauai Dining

Lihue

Gaylord's at Kilohana ✓✓✓

Kilohana Plantation
3-2087 Kaumualii Hwy (Hwy 50)
Lihue, HI 96766
808-245-9593
www.gaylordskauai.com

Hours: Bru 9:00 AM-2:00 PM Su
L 11:00 AM-2:00 PM XSu
D from 5:30 PM XSu
Cards: AE MC V
Dress: Resort Casual
Style: American/Continental/Hawaii Regional $$$

Menu Sampler: Kids Menu Too

Breakfast:
Buffet with tour reservations only - Call for details.
Sunday Brunch: Penne Alla Puttanesca served with garlic toast $14.95, Flame Broiled Hawaiian Au'ku with sunrise papaya and sweet basil butter sauce, steamed jasmine rice, garden vegetables $14.95, Chef Andy's Okinawan Sweet Potato hash with local purple sweet potato and chicken breast, two poached eggs and Maltaise sauce $13.95, Yellowfin Caesar Salad with parmesan chips $14.95
Lunch:
Appetizers: Onion Soup Gratinee $8.95, Crab & Artichoke Dip $10.95
Entrées: Jambalaya Fettucine with garlic toast $9.95, Kilohana Meat Loaf with home-made mashed potatoes, corn relish, brown butter sauce $8.95
Dinner:
Appetizers: Won Ton Wrapped Prawns with wasabi plum sauce $9.95
Entrées: Crusted Sea Bass with macadamia nut crust, banana pineapple chutney, Okinawan purple potato, lilikoi carrots, garden vegetable $25.95, Farm Raised Venison on mascarpone & white truffle polenta, wild mushrooms in raspberry mango chutney sauce, baby lilikoi carrots, garden vegetables $31.95
Adult Beverages: Beer/Wine Cellar/Cocktails – Corkage Fee $20.00

Impressions: Time Warp

Gaylord's is as much an event as a restaurant. The operation runs on the grounds of a grand old plantation where shops, carriage rides and a train have been added to the dining venue mix. This doesn't mean that the kitchen's focus was diverted. Quite the contrary! The courtyard dining area serves an impressive array of truly complex cuisine from a menu with an identity of its own. We view the approach as global fusion mélange. Consider this experience gracious, genteel or romantic.

Lihue

Genki Sushi ✓✓

Kukui Grove Mall
3-2600 Kaumualii Hwy (Hwy 50)
Lihue, HI 96766
808-632-2450
www.genkisushiusa.com
Hours: LD 11:00 AM-9:00 PM Su-Th
LD 11:00 AM-10:00 PM Fr-Sa
Cards: AE DC DIS JCB MC V
Dress: Casual
Style: Japanese/Kaiten Sushi $

Menu Sampler:

Small Plates/Kids

Breakfast:
N/A
Lunch/Dinner:
Gold Plates: for $1.55 include Natto Maki, Oshinko Maki, Kinoko Mushroom, Ocean Salad, California Roll, Miso Soup, Shisamo, Soybean, Inari, Canadian Roll, Tako, Ika, Tamago, Tuna Salad, Hot Dog Maki, Ume Maki, Corn, Kampyo Maki, Avocado Maki, Kappa Maki, Nishiki Roll, Vegetable Croquette, Tofu, Shishamo, Soybean (Edamame), Toss Salad
Green Plates: for $2.20 include Ahi Poke, Scallop Mayo, Tekka Maki, Spicy Tuna, Tobiko, Vegetarian Inside-out Roll, Seafood Salad, Negitoro, Mochi Ice Cream, Green Tea Ice Cream, Oreo Ice Cream Cookie
Red Plates: for $2.85 include Unagi, Hamachi, Ahi, Amaebi, Ebi, Fresh Salmon, Yaki Salmon, Chicken Karaage, Saba, Tako Karaage, Teriyaki Chicken Bowl, Unagi Maki, Crab Mayo, Chawan Mushi, Salmon Skin Maki
Silver Plates: for $3.95 include Ebi Fry, Salmon Sashimi, and Dragon Roll
Black Plates: for $4.90 include Ahi Sashimi, Rainbow Roll, Soft Shell Maki
Bentos, Genki Sets & Party Platters: available for $4.50 to $29.90
Adult Beverages: BYOB - No Corkage Fee But Must Finish Bottle

Impressions:

Conveyor Sushi

People from around the world enjoy proper sushi and low prices. Unfortunately it's hard to find the two together. Genki Sushi takes a fast food approach to this dilemma making a credible attempt at combining authenticity with affordability. Guests are seated around a moving conveyor system that transports color-coded plates for all to choose from. Diners take their selections off the track then stack their finished plates for pricing at check-out. It might not be a sushi purist's idea of perfection, but its all good fun at a cost that's affordable regardless of budget.

Kauai Dining

West Side

Grinds Café & Espresso ✓✓

Ele'ele Shopping Center
4469 Waialo Road
Ele'ele, HI 96705
808-335-6027
www.grindscafe.net
Hours: BLD 6:00 AM-9:00 PM
Cards: AE DIS DC JCB MC V
Dress: Casual
Style: American/Local/Bakery $

Menu Sampler: Kids Menu Too

Breakfast:
Skillets include rice or potatoes and are served all day. Portuguese Skillet with grilled Portuguese sausage, onions and green peppers with white cheeses $7.50, Farmers Skillet with homemade sausage grilled with green peppers and onions smothered with homemade country gravy $7.50, Omelets are served with rice or potatoes. Chili & Cheddar Cheese Omelet $6.95, Smoked Turkey, Mushrooms and Monterey Jack Cheese Omelet $6.50, Mahi Mahi Breakfast of grilled mahi, choice of rice or potatoes and two eggs any style $7.50, Loco Moco $6.50

Lunch:
Sandwiches: All come with condiments and choice of bread. Italian Sandwich $6.50, Super Veggie Sandwich $6.00, Cajun Ono Sandwich $7.00, Crispy Chicken Sandwich w/grilled mushrooms, jack cheese, Dijon mustard $7.00
Salads: Chicken Walnut Salad topped with hot sliced chicken slices $9.75
Pizza: 12", 15" and 18", Wheat or white crust with a wide variety of toppings Sicilian $16.50/$19.50/$26.00, Veggie $16.00/$19.00/$24.00, Cajun Chicken $16.00/$19.50/$25.00, Canadian Bacon Pineapple $15.00/$18.00/$22.00

Dinner:
Mahi Mahi lightly breaded, grilled and served with homemade tartar sauce, rice and choice of mac salad or cole slaw $8.25, Cajun Ono with sides $7.50
Pastas: Cajun Chicken Linguine with green peppers, onions, celery, carrots and Cajun Sauce $14.50, Veggie and Pesto Linguine $12.50, add Ono $3.50
Espresso: Latte, Cappuccino, Americano, Mocha, Soy Milk, Black Mountain
Adult Beverages: Beer/Wine

Impressions: Hearty Fare

Grinds is an affordable little place along the highway on the way to the Waimea Canyon. This home-style eatery does it all—breakfast, lunch and dinner. Parties with lots of different tastes will find something for everybody in this casual café.

Hamura Saimin Stand ✓✓✓

2956 Kress Street
Lihue, HI 96766
808-245-3271
Web: None
Hours: LD 10:00 AM-11:00 PM Mo-Th
LD 10:00 AM-1:00 AM Fr-Sa
LD 10:00 AM-9:30 PM Su
Cards: None
Dress: Casual
Style: Island $

Menu Sampler:

Breakfast:
N/A
Lunch/Dinner:
Saimin noodle soup with garnishes of green onions, fish cake and chopped ham in small $4.25, medium $4.50, large $4.75 and ex-large $5.25, Wun Tun Mein Saimin with pork and shrimp filled dumplings $5.75, Special Saimin $6.00, Extra Large Special Saimin $7.00, Shrimp Saimin with two pieces deep fried tempura shrimp $6.00, Extra garnishes $1.35 each, BBQ Sticks grilled chicken or beef skewers dipped in teriyaki sauce $1.40 each, Udon $4.75, Fried Noodles $4.50, Lilikoi Chiffon Pie $2.25/piece or $12.00/pie, Pretzels $2.00, Soda $.85, Bottled Water $1.30, Malasadas available on Mo, We, Fr and Sa 2/$1.00
Adult Beverages: N/A

Impressions: Island Icon

Traveling through time to Old Hawaii is an everyday occurrence at Hamura's Saimin Stand. Take your place at the diminutive counter lined with stools that zigzags back and forth across the front of this plantation-era building. Then let the ladies dish you up an order of the best local style noodle soup you've ever tasted. Don't be shy about sitting down next to another customer and "talking story". Everyone is friendly and will offer advice about how to best enjoy the hot mustard and other condiments. Order a BBQ stick and you're on your way to living local. One word of caution though, only Hawaiians and teenage boys have enough stamina to finish an extra large bowl of saimin so consider something smaller. The lilikoi chiffon pie is a signature item so why not give that a try? This cultural icon can get very crowded around mealtime. We like to stop by during off-times when parking is less of an issue. The shop is in a business area of Lihue that's down a side-street so look at a map before starting the car.

Kauai Dining

North Shore

Hanalei Dolphin Restaurant ✓✓✓
5-5016 Kuhio Hwy (Hwy 56)
Hanalei, HI 96714
808-826-6113
www.hanaleidolphin.com
Hours: L 11:30 AM-3:00 PM
D 5:30 PM-10:00 PM
Cards: MC V
Dress: Casual
Style: Seafood/Steak $$$

Menu Sampler: Kids Menu Too

Breakfast:
N/A
Lunch:
Fin Burger charbroiled or Cajun $Market, Bull Burger w/salad or fries $10.95, Calamari Sandwich deep-fried, lettuce, tomato and onion $9.95, Fish & Chips w/fries $13.95, Main Dish Salads $8.95-$13.95, Seafood Chowder $4.00/$8.00
Salads: Various Greens, Chinese Cabbage, Bean Sprouts, Tomatoes with Chicken or Calamari $11.95, with Grilled Fish, charbroiled or Cajun $13.95
Dinner:
Appetizers: Artichoke Crowns stuffed with garlic, butter, bread crumbs and cheese $8.95, Ceviche of raw fish marinated in lemon juice with tomatoes, celery, chili, Chinese parsley and green olives $7.95, Sashimi Plate $Market
Entrées: All entrées are served with a family style salad and house dressing, penne pasta, steak fries, rice or marinated veggie kabob and hot homemade bread. Fresh Scallops baked in wine, smothered in mozzarella $28.95, Hawaiian Chicken breast marinated in soy sauce and ginger $22.95/child's plate $18.95, Filet Mignon $28.00, Fish 'n Chips $23.95, Australian Lobster Tails 20-24 oz. $Market, Fresh Fish Our Specialty please ask your waiter for details $Market
Desserts: Dolphin Ice Cream Pie $8.00, New York Cheesecake $6.50
Adult Beverages: Beer/Wine/Cocktails – Corkage Fee $10.00

Impressions: Riverfront Dining

For us this open-air restaurant catches the magic of the Hanalei Valley. Look for it alongside the river on the way into the village. The Dolphin is a local tradition with its tiny lights reflecting off the water. The menu avoids trendy contrivances and comes at you straight on. They have a fish market in the rear of the building so you can be sure that the catch of the day is truly fresh. A light menu is served from 3:30 to 5:30 PM. It's not cheap, but the ambiance makes its own statement.

Lihue

Hanama'ulu Restaurant ✓✓

3-4291 Kuhio Hwy (Hwy 56)
Lihue, HI 96715
808-245-2511
Web: None
Hours: L10:00 AM-1:00 PM Tu-Fr
D 5:00 PM-8:30 PM Tu-Su
D Buf 5:30 PM-8:30 PM Su
Cards: MC V
Dress: Casual
Style: Chinese/Japanese $$

Menu Sampler:

Breakfast:
N/A
Lunch:
Deluxe Chinese Plate Lunch soup, fried chicken, fried shrimp, chop suey, crisp won ton, sweet and sour spare ribs, char siu or kau yuk served with rice and tea $9.00, Japanese Special Plate Lunch includes miso soup, rice and tea and choice of calamari steak, sukiyaki with tofu, tonkatsu, teriyaki fish, teriyaki chicken, teriyaki beef, fish tempura or donburi $8.75, Won Ton Soup $8.00
Dinner:
Sunday Oriental Buffet: Adults $21.95, Children 7-12 $15.95
Pupus: Crispy Won Ton $6.00, Spring Rolls $8.50, Potstickers $8.50
Entrées: Pork and Vegetables with Tomato $9.00, Beef and Broccoli with Mushrooms $9.00, Crisp Fried Ginger Chicken $7.50, Shrimp Canton $10.50, Shrimp Tempura with traditional dipping sauce $12.00, Tofu Tempura $6.50
Complete Dinners: Family Style 9 Course Chef's Deluxe Chinese or Chef's Special Japanese Dinners $19.95 per person, Hanama'ulu Special Platter $17.50
Dessert: Azuki Tempura $4.00, Green Tea Ice Cream $3.00
Adult Beverages: Beer/Wine/Cocktails - Corkage Fee $2.50/person

Impressions: Japanese Garden

The complete name of this dining place was once the Hanama'ulu Restaurant, Tea House, Sushi Bar, and Robatayaki. Try putting that in a phone book! This rambling 80-year old restaurant can be found on the Lihue bypass across from the 7-11. Add a touch of the exotic to your evening by making a reservation in one of their traditional Japanese tatami rooms. This is a sleeper. Don't judge it by curb appeal. Diners looking for a unique experience will be glad they made the call. Park in the lot north of the building and enter on the path thru the gate.

West Side

Hanapepe Café ✓✓✓

3830 Hanapepe Road
Hanapepe, HI 96716
808-335-5011
Web: None
Hours: L 11:00 AM-3:00 PM Mo-Th
L 11:00 AM-2:00 PM Fr
D 6:00 PM-9:00 PM Fr
Cards: MC V
Dress: Casual
Style: Gourmet Vegetarian/Seafood $$

Menu Sampler:

Kids Menu Too

Breakfast:
N/A
Lunch:
Beverages: Fresh Pressed Apple Juice 1.50, Herbal iced tea 1.75, Tropical fruit smoothie 3.50, Sparkling mineral water 1.50, Espresso, Cappuccino, Lattes
Soups & Salads: Served with fresh baked focaccia bread. House Caesar 7.00, Grilled Vegetable Salad with grilled tofu 11.00, Small side salads 3.50
Specialties: Frittata baked with fresh island eggs and cream with smoked mozzarella, sautéed mushrooms and veggies 8.50, Pasta with Pesto or Marinara 9.50, Lasagna layers of seasonal vegetables between mozzarella and parmesan cheeses 9.75, other announced specials available.
Sandwiches: Served on your choice of focaccia, multi-grain, sourdough or Ezekiel bread with Kauai's own Taro Chips. Hanapepe Healthnut Sandwich hummus, Dijon, grilled onion, lettuce, tomato, cucumber, zucchini, yellow squash, red bell pepper 7.00, Garden Burger with Dijon, lettuce and tomato 6.00
Dinner:
Entrées: Penne Pasta with summer vegetables in a creamy pesto sauce 16.00, Crepes Filled Fresh Asparagus and Mushrooms accompanied by a lemon beurre blanc 20.00, Creole Bouillabaisse of local onaga, ahi, scallops and shrimp 22.00
Adult Beverages: N/A

Impressions:

Great Bakery

Here's a health-oriented vegetarian restaurant that actually works! The service is caring and the food delicious. Flavors are created through use of fresh herbs and spices rather than by adding salt or fat. Portions are substantial enough, but for a bonus save room for their homemade desserts. Hanapepe is evolving into a bit of an art colony making this a great fit. You'll find it on the old highway thru town.

East Coast

Hong Kong Café ✓✓

Wailua Shopping Plaza
4-361 Kuhio Hwy (Hwy 56)
Kapa'a, HI 96746
808-822-3288
Web: None
Hours: LD 11:00 AM-9:00 PM Mo-Fr
LD 1:00 PM-9:00 PM Sa-Su
Cards: AE MC V
Dress: Casual
Style: Chinese/Pacific $

Menu Sampler:

Breakfast:
N/A
Lunch/Dinner:
Plate Lunches: Includes two scoops Jasmine rice, one scoop macaroni salad and spicy sweet & sour cabbage. Duck with Ginger Chicken $7.95, Chicken Katsu $7.25, Roast Duck $7.95, Crispy Chicken $7.25, Lemon Chicken $7.25
Super Bentos: Crispy Chicken, Sweet & Sour Ribs, Kau Gee, Gon Lo Mein, Jasmine Rice $7.95, Beef Broccoli, Lemon Shoyu Chicken, Kau Gee, Mein, Jasmine Rice $8.50, S & S Pork, Crispy Chicken, Kau Gee, Mein, Rice $8.50
Appetizers: Deep Fried Crab & Cheese Won Ton (6 pcs) $5.75, Deep Fried Won Ton (12 pcs) $4.75, Deep Fried Kau Gee (6 pcs) $5.25, S & S Sauce $.50
Soups: Won Ton Soup $7.50, Hot & Sour Soup (vegetarian) $4.50/$7.50, Crispy Chicken Saimin $6.95, Egg Drop Soup w/veg $7.50, Scallop Soup $8.50
Entrées: Sizzling Happy Family $12.95, Shrimp with Cashew Nuts $9.50, Kung Pao Chicken $8.50, Pork with Bitter Melon & Black Bean $8.50, Roast Pork Choy Sum (Ham Ha) $8.50, Kung Pao Tofu $8.50, Beef Broccoli $7.95
Specials: Orange Garlic Beef $8.95, Sautéed Mahi Mahi with fresh basil and egg plant $13.95, Tai Pan Pasta with fresh crushed chili and garlic sauce, chicken & shrimp, julian of greens $9.50, Sweet & Sour Filet of Snapper with fresh shredded ginger $13.95, Spicy Sautéed Shrimp, herbed sauce $10.95
Adult Beverages: BYOB

Impressions: Special Storefront

This cozy little storefront features Chinese food cooked by chefs from China. Will wonders ever cease! The menu is varied and authentic, but our favorites usually appear on the specials board. Fresh island fish and homegrown herbs make their way to the kitchen daily. Stop by and enjoy this affordable dining.

North Shore

Additional Location

Java Kai Hanalei ✓

Hanalei Center
5-5183C Kuhio Hwy (Hwy 56)
Hanalei, HI 96714
808-826-6717
www.javakai.com
Hours: B 6:30 AM-6:00 PM
Cards: MC V
Dress: Casual
Style: Coffee/Specialty $

4-1384 Kuhio Hwy
Kapa'a, HI 96746
808-823-6887

Menu Sampler:

Breakfast:
A collection of pastries, traditional items and great Belgian waffles! Try their Kauai Waffle with papaya, banana, macadamia nuts and whipped cream on a fresh hot Belgian waffle for $8.75. Other treats include the Surfer's Sandwich with egg, bacon slices and cheese on an English Muffin $7.35, Granola with milk or soy $6.50, North Shore Skillet with eggs, potatoes, ham and cheese, muffin or toast $8.50, Vegetarian Skillet with veggies and jalapenos $8.50, Papaya Boat with yogurt and granola $8.25, Lattes, Smoothies and Juices
Baked Items: Aloha Bars of toasted coconut, macadamia nuts and chocolate chips on a shortbread cookie crust; bagels, smoothies, specialty flavored coffee drinks, lemon bars, homemade muffins, apple pie, chocolate chip mac nut and amazing cookies, shortbread with lemon topping, carrot cake and biscotti
Adult Beverages: N/A
Lunch/Dinner:
N/A

Impressions:

Day Starter

The first thing that strikes newcomers to Java Kai is the aroma of freshly brewed coffee. That's a great start, but these folks do a good job with their kitchen items as well. Customers order breakfast sandwiches and baked goodies at the counter for delivery to their table. Then it's time to while away a misty Hanalei morning. Nothing happens fast on this side of Kauai so take it light and get into the mood.

Lihue

JJ's Broiler ✓✓

Anchor Cove Shopping Plaza
3416 Rice Street
Lihue, HI 96766
808-246-4422
www.jjsbroiler.com
Hours: L 11:00 AM-5:00 PM
D 5:00 PM-9:00 PM
Cards: DC DIS JCB MC V
Dress: Casual
Style: American/Pacific Rim $$$

Menu Sampler:

Kids Menu Too

Breakfast:
N/A
Lunch:
Hawaiian Ocean Chowder $7.99, French Onion Soup $7.99, Fish & Chips with seasoned fries and malt vinegar $15.99, Asian Grilled Chicken Salad with crisp vegetables and rice noodles served with hoisin dressing and a grilled chicken breast $13.99, Philly Steak Sandwich w/rice or fries and pickle $11.99, Sautéed Mushroom Cheeseburger w/rice or fries and pickle $11.49, Rueben $11.99
Dinner:
Appetizers, Salads & Soups: Onion Soup w/glazed cheese and onion $7.79, Clam Bucket - 2 lbs in white wine, garlic, herbs $20.99, JJ's Escargot $11.99, Shrimp Scampi w/garlic & mushrooms served on saffron rice noodles $15.99
Entrées: All entrées include table salad bar & choice of steamed or house rice. Roasted Macadamia Lamb Rack with juniper garlic sauce $27.99, Prime Rib of Beef with au jus and horseradish $29.99, Coconut Shrimp with curried coconut crumbs, mango sauce and chutney $23.99, Lobster Tail Fettucine with shitake mushrooms, basil, in garlic cream sauce $39.99 , Spicy Wasabi New York Steak with a spicy wasabi crust $30.95, JJ's World Famous Slavonic Steak of broiled filet sliced thin and dipped in a special butter, wine and garlic sauce $26.95
Adult Beverages: Beer/Wine/Cocktails – Corkage Fee $10.00

Impressions:

Kauai Favorite

You'll find JJ's Broiler near the Marriott overlooking the beach on Nawiliwili Bay. Casual meals are served downstairs either inside or out on the lanai with the second floor open for dinner. Portions are quite generous, so sharing is an option. After work a lively crowd gathers in the lounge to enjoy their favorite adult beverages and relive the day's events. The plaza provides a lot out front.

South Shore

Joe's On The Green ✓✓

Kiahuna Golf Club
2545 Kiahuna Plantation Drive
Koloa, HI 96756
808-742-9696
Web: None
Hours: B 7:00 AM-11:30 AM
L 11:30 AM-2:30 PM
Cards: MC V
Dress: Casual
Style: American/Island $

Menu Sampler:

Kids Menu Too

Breakfast:
Breakfast Specials include choice of hash browns or rice. Eggs Benedict $10.75, Create your own 3-egg omelet $9.50, Caroline's Breakfast Burrito flour tortilla, beans, scrambled eggs, salsa, cheese, olives & sour cream $9.50, French Toast $8.25, Banana Macadamia Nut Pancakes $8.95, Tropical Mix Granola $4.95, Continental Joe with fresh fruit, pastry or toast and choice of beverage $8.50

Lunch:
"Personalized" House Salad served with a focaccia breadstick $8.75, New England Style Seafood Chowder cup $3.95, with a half turkey or tuna sandwich $8.50, with a small house salad $8.25, or a bowl of chowder $5.95. Sandwiches are served with French fries, island coleslaw, potato-mac salad or steamed rice. Joe's Mama Burger $8.50, Chicken Avocado with jack cheese, grilled $9.75. Lunch Specials include Fish and Chips w/cole slaw & fries $10.25, Linguini with Chicken-Artichoke Sausage & vegetables $9.50, Chicken Cutlet served with sautéed veggie's, rice & gravy $8.95, Loco Moco 1/3# hamburger $6.95

Desserts: Lilikoi Dream Ice Cream Pie $4.95, Kauai Ice Cream Pie $4.95

Dinner:
N/A

Adult Beverages: Beer/Wine/Cocktails – Corkage Fee $8.00

Impressions:

Fun Breakfast

This popular dining spot is located in the golf course clubhouse at the beautiful Kiahuna Plantation. Going by the informal moniker of Joe's On The Green this establishment offers an affordable upscale alternative for residents and visitors alike. If you've noticed birds trying to snatch a morsel at the island restaurants, wait until you see the native moa chickens engage in a war of wits with the fast footed, squirt bottle packing waitresses at Joe's. "Hey, they live on Kauai too!"

West Side

Kalaheo Café & Coffee Co ✓✓

2-2560 Kaumualii Hwy (Hwy 50)
Kalaheo, HI 96741
808-332-5858
www.kalaheo.com

Hours: Br 6:30 AM-2:00 PM Su
B 6:30 AM-11:30 AM Mo-Sa
L 11:30 AM-2:30 PM
D From 5:30 PM-8:30 PM We-Sa
Cards: MC V
Dress: Casual
Style: American/Family $$

Menu Sampler: Kids Menu Too

Breakfast:
Pancakes $5.25, w/seasonal fruit $7.50, Bonzo Burrito Tortilla Wrap w/sautéed ham, peppers, mushrooms, onions, olives and black beans scrambled with two eggs, wrapped in a burrito with cheddar and Monterey jack $8.25, Three item omelettes with white or brown rice, café fries or hash browns and toast $8.95
Beverages: Café Au Lait, Red Eye, Black Eye, Espresso Americano, Hot Chocolate, Spiced Chai, Iced Coffee, Cappucino, Latte, Mocha
Lunch:
Sandwiches Include soup, potato salad, green salad or cilantro garlic fries. Hot Pastrami Kalaheo Style with grilled onions, mushrooms, Swiss Cheese on fresh baked bread $8.95, Grilled Pesto Chicken $10.95, Soup, Salad & Focaccia $8.95
Dinner:
Appetizers: BBQ Baby Back Pork Ribs $9.95, Today's Fresh Soup $4.95
Salads: Garden Greens with Fresh Catch $15.95, Kalaheo Field Greens $6.25
Entrées: Grilled Fresh Fish Melt $12.95, Freshly Made Turkey Burger $11.25, Hunan Style Grilled Pork Tenderloin $18.95, Orange-Bourbon Glazed Half Chicken with pineapple slaw, smashed potato $17.25, Grilled NY Steak $26.50
Adult Beverages: Beer/Wine – Corkage Fee Varies

Impressions: Roadside Rest

Kalaheo Café & Coffee Co has grown from a order-yourself-at-the-counter kind of place to a full service restaurant with a menu that's taken on a feel of its own. Today's visitors will find reasonably priced breakfast and lunch offerings along with dinner selections that recently came up on their radar screen. The mom and pop ambiance is secure with a friendly staff and pleasant surroundings. Consider including this stop when taking a road trip to Barking Sands or Waimea Canyon.

West Side

Kalaheo Steak House ✓✓✓

4444 Papalina Road
Kalaheo, HI 96741
808-332-7217
Web: None
Hours: D 5:00 PM-9:30 PM
Cards: MC V
Dress: Resort Casual
Style: Steak & Seafood $$$

Menu Sampler: Kids Menu Too

Breakfast/Lunch:
N/A
Dinner:
Appetizers: Steamer Clams (when available) $13.95, Shrimp Cocktail $12.95, Sautéed Mushrooms $10.95, Teriyaki Beef Sticks marinated and broiled $10.95
Entrées: All dinners include house salad with white rice, bread and butter. Top Sirloin $21.95, with a teriyaki marinade $22.95, New York $27.95, Rib Eye $26.95, Tenderloin topped with sautéed mushrooms $26.95, Prime Rib slow roasted with au jus gravy and blended horseradish sauce $25.95/$33.95, Teriyaki Split Broiler marinated in house teriyaki sauce and broiled with a slice of pineapple $18.95, Barbecue Chicken Breast $20.95, Baby Back Pork Ribs roasted then flame broiled with sauce $21.95, Rack of Lamb $Market Price, Kalaheo Shrimp sautéed in butter, lemon and fresh garlic topped with parmesan and parsley and served on white rice $25.95, Alaskan King Crab Legs $Market Price , Mahimahi Fillet $Market Price, Lobster Tail $Market Price
Side Orders: House Soup $8.95, Mixed Greens $8.95, Baked Potato $3.95
Desserts: Chocolate Sundae $4.95, Waffle Sundae $5.95
Adult Beverages: Beer/Wine/Cocktails

Impressions: Country Clubhouse

Kalaheo Steak House has the friendly atmosphere you expect to find in a small town dining spot. However, as soon as you open the menu you're back on Main Street. This restaurant offers a metropolitan steak and seafood menu without the usual big-city prices. To find this little gem drive a few miles south from Poipu Beach to Kalaheo and take a left at the stoplight on Papalina Road. Then go one block, look on your left, and you're there. A small parking area is located at the far side of the building backed up with plenty of open curbside along the street.

Lihue

Kalapaki Beach Hut ✓✓

Nawiliwili Bay
3474 Rice Street
Lihue, HI 96766
808-246-6330
Web: None
Hours: B 7:00 AM-10:30 AM
LD 10:30 AM-8:00 PM Tu-Su
LD 10:30 AM-9:00 PM Mo
Cards: MC V
Dress: Casual
Style: American/Island $

Menu Sampler:

Kids Menu Too

Breakfast:
Breakfast Egg Sandwich (served all day) Bacon or Portuguese Sausage, Egg, Cheese with lettuce and tomato 4.75 green chilies add .55, Sweet Bread French Toast 4.95, Beach Hut Choice of ono with two eggs, toast and choice of rice or hash browns 6.95, Omelettes with 3 eggs and choice of fillings 5.75 to 7.75

Lunch/Dinner:
Burgers: all prepared with lettuce, tomato, onion and mayonnaise, Beach Burger ¼ # 4.50, Cheeseburger (Cheddar or Swiss) 5.25, Aloha Burger 4.90, Blue Cheeseburger 5.50, Delicious Buffalo or Blank Angus Burgers add 2.50 to any of the above, add jalapenos, green chilies or teriyaki to any burger .65 each
Sandwiches: Tuna Melt 5.75, Teriyaki Chicken, Ono Charbroiled Fish 6.50, Mushroom Melt w/cheese 6.95, Natural Burger garden burger w/the works 5.95
Fish & Chips: Battered fish served with house tartar sauce, lemon wedges, malt vinegar and basket of fries, Small 4.50, Large 6.50
Salads & Sides: Garden Salad w/papaya seed or ranch 4.95, Caesar Classic 5.25, with chicken or ono 7.95, French Fries, Regular 1.95, Large 2.50
Beverages: Passion Orange Guava (POG) 2.25, Soft Drinks 1.75, Coffee 1.45
Adult Beverages: N/A

Impressions:

Open-Air

Those traveling the bargain trail will find a welcome stop at the Kalapaki Beach Hut. This is the kind of place many look for but seldom find. Here in the middle of the usual commercial clutter you can sit out in reach of a beautiful beach and enjoy breakfast, lunch, or dinner without losing your shirt. Food quality is a big plus. Sure, the menu's on the simple side, but isn't that what being at a beach is all about? Orders are prepared one at a time, so relax 'cause you're on vacation!

East Coast

Additional Lo

Kauai Pasta ✓✓✓

4-939B Kuhio Hwy (Hwy 56)
Kapa'a, HI 96746
808-822-7447
Web: None
Hours: D 5:00 PM-9:00 PM XMo
Cards: MC V
Dress: Resort Casual
Style: Italian $$

3142 Kuhio Hwy
Lihue, HI 96766
808-245-2227

Menu Sampler:

Kids Menu Too

Breakfast:
N/A
Lunch:
Served at Lihue location only; call for additional information.
Dinner:
Salads: Salads are served with homemade garlic bread. Add grilled chicken to any salad $3.50. House Salad with baby greens $6.95, Classic Caesar $5.95
Panini Sandwiches: All are served with Caesar of Baby Greens side salad. Mushroom Panini with fresh mozzarella, pesto, Island Tomatoes $10.95
Pasta: All pasta dishes are served with homemade garlic bread. Choice of Spaghetti or Fettuccini. House Pasta Sauce, a Bolognese Style meat sauce with Italian sausage, Black Angus beef & mushrooms $9.95, Fettuccini Alfredo with parmesan & cream $10.95, The Sampler w/marinara, pesto and Alfredo $11.95
Entrées: All are served with homemade garlic bread. Manicotti shells filled with three cheeses, herbs & spices $7.95/$12.95, add House meat sauce $1.00/ $2.00, Chicken Parmesan $14.95, Eggplant Parmesan $13.95, Italian Herb Grilled Shrimp marinated tiger shrimp in garlic, olive oil, fresh basil, with Fettuccini Alfredo $15.95, Pesto Grilled Chicken Breast w/Alfredo $12.95
Dessert: Tiramisu Cheesecake $6.95, Dark Chocolate Crème Brulee $6.95
Take-Out Special: Pasta Dinner for Four, Sauce, Salad, Bread $38.95
Adult Beverages: Beer/Wine – Corkage Fee $10.00

Impressions:

Island Hip

There's a lot to like about this happy little place. First, unlike many of the island eateries, there's actually plenty of room to park! Then, guests are welcomed into a cozy room warmed with booths and Tuscan colors. The creative menu follows suit reaching out beyond what is normally found at a typical pasta house. Before ordering, listen while the server recites the daily specials. The chef-owners keep the regulars interested by mixing things up. Try lunch at the new Lihue location.

South Shore

Keoki's Paradise ✓✓

Poipu Shopping Village
2360 Kiahuna Plantation Drive
Koloa, HI 96756
808-742-7535
www.keokisparadise .com
Hours: L 11:00 AM-11:00 PM
D 5:00 PM-10:00 PM
Cards: AE DC DIS JCB MC V
Dress: Resort Casual
Style: Steak/Seafood/Island $$

Menu Sampler:

Kids Menu Too

Breakfast:
N/A

Lunch:

Plate Lunch: w/two scoop rice, Koloa Pork Ribs $9.95, Grilled Island Fresh Fish $12.95, Hawaiian Fish and Chips $9.95, Stir-Fry Chicken Cashew $9.95, Veggie and Cashew Stir Fry $8.95, Bamboo Special $Market Price
Sandwiches: Keoki's Fish Sandwich $11.95, Keoki's Paradise Burger $7.95, Cheeseburger $8.50, Tuna & Cheddar $6.95, Grilled Roast Beef & Cheddar $7.95. Cobb Salad $9.95, Grilled Chicken Caesar Salad $10.95. Nachos $6.95

Dinner:

Pupus: Thai Shrimp Sticks grilled and served with a tangy guava cocktail sauce $9.95, Panko Crusted Scallops with Wasabi Butter Sauce $9.95.
Fish: Prepared five different ways, baked or sautéed w/sauces $21.95 to $25.95
Entrées: All entrées are served w/Keoki's Caesar Salad and a basket of freshly baked bread. Coconut Crusted Chicken with coconut & mango sauce $15.95, Prime Rib $21.95/$29.95, Koloa Pork Ribs Asian Style glazed with plum sauce $18.95, Pesto Shrimp Macadamia over rice pilaf $17.95
Adult Beverages: Beer/Wine – Corkage Fee $10.00

Impressions:

Hawaiiana Kitsch

Anyone in search of bamboo, torches, umbrella drinks, and live Hawaiian music should love Keoki's Paradise. This is Hawaii as it never really was except in the minds of Hollywood set designers. Who cares? It's fun anyway. After the drinks are served you'll be presented with a menu featuring old-time favorites prepared with tropical spins. Servings are usually generous and come at reasonable prices. This combination attracts a lively crowd and makes for a good time. Keoki's is a large place with lots of parking. The long hours make this a great late-night stop.

North Shore

Kilauea Bakery & Pau Hana Pizza ✓✓✓

Kong Lung Center
2484 Keneke Street
Kilauea, HI 96754
808-828-2020
Web: None
Hours: Bakery 6:30 AM-9:00 PM
Pizza 11:00 AM-9:00 PM
Cards: MC V
Dress: Casual
Style: Pastry/Coffee/Pizza $

Menu Sampler:

Breakfast:
Coffee made by the cup in the bakery with scones and sweet cinnamon buns. Breakfast pastries and Danishes use mac nuts, mango, cream cheese, lilikoi, coconut and papaya flavors. Full service gourmet coffee and espresso bar.

Lunch/Dinner:
Tuscan Style Pizza served as traditional or as gourmet whole or by the slice. Sizes are small 10", medium 12" and large 16" ranging in price from \$9.65 to \$30.35. Specialty Pizzas are small \$14.85, medium \$20.85 and large \$28.10 and are wonderful gourmet combinations such as Pomodoro, fresh tomatoes, Kilauea goat cheese, house marinated artichokes, black olives and mozzarella cheese, or the Billie Holliday of smoked ono, spinach, roasted onions, gorgonzola rosemary sauce and mozzarella cheese, Provencal, Pesto Mystic, Scampi

Soup & Salad: Kailani Farms organic lettuce blend, carrots, purple cabbage, tomato, organic sunflower sprouts and crispy croutons \$7.95, add BBQ Chicken \$3.75 or Pau Hana Smoked Ono \$4.25, Three Homemade Soups Daily

Adult Beverages: N/A

Impressions: Truly Fresh

Take the turn-off from the Kuhio Highway to the Kilauea National Marine and Wildlife Reserve and you will find yourself in the simple north shore village of Kilauea. Follow the road out toward the Kilauea Lighthouse until you reach the Kong Lung Center. There in the garden courtyard resides the Kilauea Bakery & Pau Hana Pizza. This is a very popular place with the locals—they line up in the morning with their coffee cups in hand. You'll know why when your eyes start to shine after the first cup! The pastries are an excellent accompaniment to their specialty coffees and teas. Lunch and dinner guests find the pizzas to be hearty, authentic, and delicious. There are a few small tables available for onsite dining.

East Coast

King and I Thai Cuisine ✓✓

4-901 Kuhio Hwy (Hwy 56)
Kapa'a, HI 96746
808-822-1642
Web: None
Hours: D 4:30 PM-9:00 PM
Cards: AE DC MC V
Dress: Resort Casual
Style: Thai $$

Menu Sampler:

Breakfast/Lunch:
N/A
Dinner:
Appetizers: Siam Mee Koab $7.50, Spring Rolls $8.50, Crispy Calamari $8.50, Sa~Teh, with barbeque chicken $9.95, with shrimp or fish $11.50
Salads & Soups: Green Papaya Salad $7.95, Beef Salad $9.50, Siam Chicken Coconut Soup $8.50, Spicy Lemongrass Soup with shrimp or fish $9.50
Rice: Siam Fried Rice with shrimp $10.95, with beef, pork or chicken $8.95, Sweet White Rice (Sticky) Rice $3.00, Brown Rice $2.75, White Rice $2.50
Noodles: Pork or Chicken Pad Thai $8.95, Shrimp Broccoli Noodles $10.95
Specialties: Siam Fresh Basil Beef $9.95, Siam Sweet and Sour Pork $9.95, Siam Chicken Eggplant $9.95, Siam Calamari Broccoli $9.95, Shrimp or Fish Sambal $12.95, Beef Sambal $10.95, Ginger Fish $11.95, Garlic Shrimp $11.95
Curries: Siam Fish Red Curry $11.95, Siam Pork Green Curry $9.95, Siam Chicken Yellow Curry $9.95, all can be prepared mild, medium, or hot
Vegetarian Specials: Siam Crispy Noodles $7.50, Coconut Vegetable Soup $8.50, Eggplant w/Tofu $9.95, Vegetarian Fried Rice $8.50, Basil Tofu $9.95
Desserts: Tapioca w/Coconut Milk $2.50, Black Rice w/Coconut Milk $2.75
Adult Beverages: Beer/Wine – Corkage Fee $10.00

Impressions: Daily Specials

We've often said that you could take most of the Thai menus in use, mix them in a pile, pass them out at random, and no one would know the difference. They are that similar. What makes King & I Thai Cuisine stand apart is their uncommonly solid list of daily specials. In fact, we prefer to by-pass the standards and fashion our entire meal around that listing. In all likelihood the person taking your order will be one of the owners. They're extremely knowledgeable. You'll find it hard to go wrong following their advice. Don't let the simple outside appearance fool you. It's our view that this is one of the better Thai dining experiences on Kauai.

West Side

Kokee State Park Lodge ✓

3600 Kokee Road
Kekaha, HI 96752
808-335-6061
Web: None
Hours: BL 9:00 AM-3:00 PM
Cards: AE DC DIS MC V
Dress: Casual
Style: American/Island $

Menu Sampler:

Breakfast:
Local Breakfast scrambled eggs, Portuguese sausage and rice or toast 6.75, French Toast $6.95, Pancakes $6.95, Kokee Pancake Sandwich $7.50
Lunch:
Salads & Snacks: Greek Salad w/Kalamata olives, tomato, feta cheese, marinated garbanzo beans, artichoke hearts w/vinaigrette dressing 7.75, Apple Salad w/blue cheese, mac nuts, raisins w/Lilikoi wasabi dressing 7.75, House Salad w/Lilikoi wasabi dressing 4.75, Corn Bread 3.50, Banana Bread 3.25, Crab Shumai with plum sauce $4.95, Chicken Wings with house salad 6.95
Soups & Dishes: Chili 6.75, Chili & Rice 7.75, Quiche spinach, cheese & Portuguese sausage 6.95, Portuguese Bean Soup 6.25, Clam Chowder 6.25
Sandwiches: Kokee Club 7.95, Tuna with lettuce, tomatoes & mayo on whole grain bread 6.95, Turkey w/lettuce, tomatoes mayo & Lilikoi mustard on whole grain bread 6.95, Ham w/lettuce, tomatoes, mayo & Lilikoi wasabi mustard on whole grain bread 6.95, Cheese, your choice of Swiss, provolone or Cheddar, grilled or cold 6.95, PBJ w/guava jelly 3.25, Kalua Pork imu roasted 6.95, BBQ Pork Hawaiian style roasted pork in tangy BBQ sauce on sesame seed bun 6.95
Desserts: Lilikoi Chiffon Pie with whip cream 3.75, Homemade Coconut Pie served warm 3.75, Carrot Cake 2.75, and Haagen-Dazs Ice Cream Bars 2.88
Adult Beverages: Beer/Wine/Cocktails
Dinner:
N/A

Impressions: Comfort Stop

Visitors to Kokee State Park come looking for wilderness at the end of the road. The menu at the lodge fits right in. There's nothing pretentious about this table! Here you fill-up on simple fare or have a snack before heading out for the day's activities. This might be the only choice around, but the prices won't blow your budget. Remember this is upcountry and can be cool and wet so come prepared.

East Coast

Kountry Style Kitchen ✓

1485 Kuhio Hwy (Hwy 56)
Kapa'a, HI 96746
808-822-3511
Web: None
Hours: B 6:00 AM-1:30 PM
L 11:00 AM-1:30 PM
Cards: MC V
Dress: Casual
Style: American/Hawaiian $

Menu Sampler:

Kids Menu Too

Breakfast:
Ham & Cheese Omelette with hash browns or rice, toast & jelly or cornbread $8.25, 8 oz. Steak & Eggs with hashed browns or rice, toast & jelly or cornbread $12.25, Omelette Bar $5.75 plus $2.50 for meats, $2.00 for cheese and $1.75 for veggies, 3 Banana or Strawberry Pancakes $6.75, French Toast $6.25, Fresh Chilled Papaya $3.25, Loco Moco $7.00, Eggs Benedict with hash browns or rice $9.25, Garden Benedict with mushrooms, spinach, tomatoes and olives served with hash browns or rice $10.00, Keiki Specials $4.50 to $4.75
Lunch:
All burgers are served with Krispy Fries. Burger Bar $6.00 plus mushrooms & bacon $1.75 each, plus cheese $1.25, plus veggies $1.00 each, BLT or Patty Melt served with French fries or potato salad $7.25, Grilled Mahi Mahi with vegetables, rice or fries, tartar sauce and hot corn bread $9.25, Kountry Fried Chicken (3 pcs) with rice or fries, vegetables and hot corn bread $10.25, Sirloin Steak Lunch $11.50, Chef Salad $8.25, Soup of the Day $2.25/$4.75
Adult Beverages: Beer/Wine
Dinner:
N/A

Impressions:

Coffee Shop

The Kountry Style Kitchen Restaurant is a classic small town coffee shop set in the middle of the Pacific. This version is located in a roadside storefront on the north end of Kapa'a. Inside customers pack the booths and tables as waitresses weave thru with coffee pots held high. A handwritten specials board completes the scene. The atmosphere is comfortable and welcoming helped along by their homey menu offerings. Quality ingredients are used and the solid plates deliver as intended. As this is just about in the center of Kauai's single highway system those doing the full island transit should find it to be a conveniently placed stop.

Lihue

LaBamba Mexican Restaurant ✓✓

Kukui Grove Mall
3-2600 Kaumualii Hwy (Hwy 50)
Lihue, HI 96766
808-245-5972
Web: None
Hours: LD 11:00 AM-9:00 PM
Cards: MC V
Dress: Casual
Style: Mexican $$

Menu Sampler:

Breakfast:
N/A
Lunch/Dinner:
Aperitivos: Nachos 7.95, add Chicken or Beef 8.95, add shredded pork 9.95, Quesadillas 5.95, Quesadillas Max with Chicken or Beef 6.95, Potato Skins 6.95
Ensaladas: Seafood Salad on a Shell 9.95, Taco Salad Grande Shell 8.95
LaBamba Ala Carta: Chicken Specialty Burrito 6.95, Carnitas Burrito 7..95, Taquitos Rico 7.95, Burrito Ala Carta 5.95, Veggie Burrito 6.95, Burrito Verde 7.95, Taco chicken or beef 3.00, Enchilada chicken, beef or cheese 3.25
Burritos: All served with rice or beans, Burrito Verde 10.95, Burrito Con Carne with shredded beef 9.95, Burrito Con Pollo (chicken) 9. 95, Chimichanga 10.95
Plates: Include rice and beans. Carnitas of tender marinated pork 12.95, Tostada Max 8.95, Enchiladas 8.95, Enchiladas Suiza covered with a rich, creamy sauce 9.95, Tacos two grande tacos, chicken or beef 8.95, Enchilada and Taco Combo with chicken or beef and served with rice or beans 9.95
Combination Plate: Choose from any two of these dishes: taco, burrito, tamale, enchilada, or chile relleno with rice and beans 14.95. Guacamole side 3.00
Desserts: Flan when available 3.50
Adult Beverages: Beer/Wine/Cocktails

Impressions: Mall Cantina

LaBamba started out as your typical family-owned Mexican restaurant in small town America. Somewhere along the line they got uprooted by redevelopment and found themselves in the nearby mall. Somehow it worked. The dining room might lack the formula look, but isn't that what you're after? All the traditional Tex-Mex favorites appear on the menu. Everything is prepared to order, so take a break and enjoy a cold one while you wait. It's worth it. Park east of the mall close to Sears and save yourself a walk. The restaurant is right by that entrance.

East Coast

Lemongrass Grill ✓✓✓

4-885 Kuhio Hwy (Hwy 56)
Kapa'a, HI 96746
808-821-2888
Web: None
Hours: D 4:00 PM-9:00 PM
Cards: AE DC DIS JCB MC V
Dress: Resort Casual
Style: Japanese/Pacific Rim $$$

Menu Sampler: Kids Menu Too

Breakfast/Lunch:
N/A
Dinner:
Starters: Golden Prawns fried in won ton wrap $8.95, Lobster Ravioli with a creamy cheese sauce $8.95, Satay Fish with a spicy peanut sauce $12.95
Salads: Lemongrass Salad with a sweet vinaigrette $7.00, Spinach Salad with a citrus island dressing $8.00, Macadamia Salad with a peanut dressing $9.50
Specialties: Sautéed Scallops with Mushrooms and a Marsala wine sauce over linguine $18.95, Rack of Lamb Loin with rosemary $25.95, Drunken Duck with a red wine sauce $18.95, Catch of the Day with béarnaise sauce $22.95, Broiled New York Steak with sautéed mushrooms $18.95, Five Spice Prime Rib $18.95, Vegetable Medley Linguine $14.95, Yellow Curry Vegetables $14.95, Steak & Prawn Scampi $25.95, Lemongrass Seafood Stew $27.95, Steamed Fish $23.95
Sushi Bar: Nigiri Sushi $3.50-$7.50, Cut Rolls: 9-1-1 of spicy tuna roll topped with avocado, katsuo bushi $9.50, Rainbow $9.50, Hand Rolls: California $4.00, Spicy Tuna $5.00, Eel $5.00, Sushi Combos: Waipoli Combo with miso soup, maguro, sake, Hamachi, Ebi, Tamago and California Roll $14.50, Viva Las Vegas Roll of tempura shrimp, crab, ahi, cucumber, deep fried and served with a sweet, spicy sauce $12.50, Spider Roll of soft shell crab and cucumber $11.50
Adult Beverages: Beer/Wine/Cocktails – Corkage Fee $15.00

Impressions: Food Fest

Our first thought upon entering Lemongrass was, "Wow! What a fabulous wood building!" Once inside you either go up the baroque staircase to the main dining room or remain downstairs at the lounge or outside on the lanai. The sushi bar is enveloped by a moat with small wood boats that were originally intended to take seafood creations to the guests. Unfortunately the corners were too tight so their boat parade ended, but the sushi keeps coming. If that course leaves you with an appetite don't miss out on the rest of the Japanese influenced Pacific Rim menu.

North Shore

Lighthouse Bistro ✓✓

Kong Lung Center
2484 Keneke Street
Kilauea, HI 96754
808-828-0480
www.lighthousebistro.com
Hours: L 12:00 PM-2:00 PM XSu
D 5:30 PM-9:00 PM
Cards: MC V
Dress: Resort Casual
Style: European/Pacific Rim $$

Menu Sampler:

Kids Menu Too

Breakfast:
N/A
Lunch:
Fish Tacos of sautéed fresh fish, tomato, onion, cilantro and seasonings in a soft shell taco & salsa $9.95, Fish Burrito with black beans and cheese $11.95, Thai Chicken Wrap w/sweet Thai chili sauce $6.95, BLT $4.95, BBQ Chicken $6.95, Cheeseburger cheddar cheese, lettuce, onion and tomato on a sesame bun $5.95, Caesar Salad with fish $15.95, Garden Burger with lettuce and tomato $6.50
Dinner:
Appetizers: Coconut Shrimp w/sweet chili sauce & aioli $13.95, Fish Rockets fish wrapped with furikake and lumpia served with a wasabi aioli $12.95
Soups & Salads: Soup Du Jour $4.95, Caesar Salad $9.95, with Fish $15.95, with Chicken $14.95, Half Caesar $6.95, Kilauea Goat Cheese Salad $14.95
Pasta: All you can eat Pasta & Sauce Bar (4 pastas, 3 sauces) $13.95
Entrées: Fresh Fish grilled with a white wine lemon beurre blanc, tropical jasmine rice pilaf and fresh vegetables $23.95, Filet Mignon Delmonico with a gorgonzola cheese burgundy sauce, mashed potatoes and vegetables $29.95, Pacific Saltimbocca veal medallions with a prosciutto gorgonzola herb sauce, mashed potatoes, vegetables $27.95, Pineapple Pork Medallions $18.95
Adult Beverages: Beer/Wine/Cocktails – Corkage Fee $10.00

Impressions:

Broad Menu

Dining options are limited on the north shore of Kauai. This sparsely populated area can only support so much. When the Lighthouse Bistro opened in Kilauea, it was a welcome addition. Not only do they serve a wide ranging dinner menu, they also offer lunch for hungry travelers. Note that the price points cover a lot of territory making this an affordable choice for assorted appetites and budgets.

Lihue

Lihue Barbecue Inn ✓✓

2982 Kress Street
Lihue, HI 96766
808-245-2921
Web: None
Hours: L 10:30 AM-1:30 PM XSu
D 5:00 PM-8:30 PM XSu
Cards: MC V
Dress: Casual
Style: American/Japanese/Local $$

Menu Sampler: Kids Menu Too

Breakfast:
N/A
Lunch:
All entrées and sandwiches include soup or fresh fruit, dessert and choice of coffee or tea. Grilled or Sautéed Fish of the Day with fruit salsa $13.95, Teriyaki Steak Sandwich $5.95, Hamburger $5.25, Katsu Donburi $9.95, Fresh Fish of the Day Sandwich with choice of slaw, fries or tossed greens $12.95
Dinner:
Specialty Salads: Peppered Ahi Salad $13.95, Seared Scallop Salad $13.95, Tempura Salmon Salad $13.95, Asian Chicken Salad $13.95

Entrées: Shrimp Scampi $18.95, Vegetarian Pasta in marinara sauce with garlic bread $13.95, Mac Nut Crusted Fresh Fish Tower with sweet chili butter sauce $23.95, Chipotle Baby Back Ribs $22.95, Baked Stuffed Mahi Mahi with snow crab, veggies & cheese, Dijon & ginger aioli $21.95, Fire Grilled Chili Prawns $19.95, Rock Salt Roasted Prime Rib of Beef au jus with horseradish sauce and baked potato $23.95, Panko Mahimahi $12.95, Assorted Tempura $15.95
Desserts: The greatest homemade cream pies come in flavors such as peanut butter, chocolate, lemon, banana, cherry, etc. at only $2.95 per slice!!
Adult Beverages: Beer/Wine/Cocktails

Impressions: Old Kauai

Years ago soldiers used to line up in the street to enjoy the Lihue Barbecue Inn's home-style food and atmosphere. Not that much has changed as a solid group of loyal customers keeps the friendly staff busy serving an extensive list of Hawaii favorites. Selections and prices cross a broad spectrum as they should in a small town like Lihue. Think all things for all people and you get the picture. The café decor includes booths and tables, but as an added twist there's a cocktail lounge.

North Shore

Mediterranean Gourmet ✓✓✓

Hanalei Colony Resort
5-7130 Kuhio Hwy (Hwy 56)
Haena, HI 96714
808-826-9875
Web: None
Hours: L 11:00AM-4:00PM XSu
D 4:00PM-9:00PM XSu
Cards: AE DC DIS JCB MC V
Dress: Resort Casual
Style: Mediterranean $$$

Menu Sampler:

Kids Menu Too

Breakfast:
N/A
Lunch:
Appetizers: Stuffed Grape Leaves $6.95, Hummus & Pita Bread $7.95
Salads: Tabouleh Salad with Hummus $12.95, Caesar Salad $8.95
Sandwiches & Wraps: Falafel Wrap (vegetarian) 11.95, Gyro Wrap w/fries $12.95, Garlic Chicken Wrap $12.95, Lettuce Wraps (low carb) $13.95, Fresh Tides Sandwich w/fries $Market, Hamburger & Fries $10.95
Entrées: Steak Kabob, hummus, pita & vegetables $21.95, Veggie Plate Lunch $16.95, Grilled Fresh Fish with rice & seasoned vegetables $Market
Dinner:
Appetizers: Hand Rolled Spinach Fatayer $7.95, Bruschetta $6.95, Grilled Kafta $8.95, Babaganush & Pita Bread $8.95, Chicken Quesadilla $9.95
Salads: Greek Salad $10.95, Summer Bliss Salad $13.95, with Fish $Market
Entrées: Veggie Plate Dinner $16.95, Steak Kabob $21.95, Rib Eye Steak $34.95, Rosemary Rack of Lamb $34.95, Mediterranean Surf & Turf $Market, Grilled Fresh Fish $Market, Seafood Medley $Market, Sunset Dinner Including Appetizer, Chicken/ Steak Kabob, Pita Bread, Hummus $25.95
Specials: Five or six high-end selections offered nightly for $30.00 to $40.00
Adult Beverages: Beer/Wine Cellar/Cocktails – Corkage Fee $5.00

Impressions:

Beachfront Bistro

North of Princeville in the Land of Hanalei you'll find that beachfront restaurant you pictured when you dreamt of the ideal Kauai vacation. Both the atmosphere and menu are genuine. Fresh herbs complement the light flavors and exceptional preparations. Seafood lovers can choose from whatever the owner caught on his morning fishing trip. It doesn't get much fresher than that --- a personal favorite!

East Coast

Mema Thai Chinese Cuisine ✓✓

Wailua Shopping Plaza
4-369 Kuhio Hwy (Hwy 56)
Kapa'a, HI 96746
808-823-0899
Web: None
Hours: L 11:00 AM-2:00 PM Mo-Fr
D 4:30 PM-9:00 PM
Cards: AE DC DIS MC V
Dress: Casual
Style: Chinese/Thai $$

Menu Sampler:

Breakfast:
N/A
Lunch/Dinner:
Appetizers: Shrimp Rolls of rice paper stuffed with long rice, onion, black mushrooms and shrimp served with lettuce, mint leaves and cucumber $7.95, Sa-teh coconut milk, peanut butter, kaffir lime leaves, seasoning, cucumber sauce on the side, choices are tofu or vegetable $7.95, Chicken on the Stick $8.95, Fish battered and deep fried $11.95, Deep Fried Shrimp $11.95
Soups: Thai Ginger Coconut Soup with kaffir lime leaves $7.95-$14.95, Long Rice Soup $7.95-$10.95, Spicy Fresh Lemongrass Soup with Shrimp $11.95
Salad: Fresh Island Papaya Salad $6.95, Calamari Salad w/lemongrass $11.95
Noodles & Rice: Pad Thai stir fried Thai rice noodles with eggs, chives and bean sprouts topped with peanuts and lemon on the side, chicken or pork $10.95, shrimp $12.95, seafood $18.95, Broccoli Noodles with Pork $9.95
Entrées: Fried Garlic Pork with garlic & black pepper served on a bed of chopped cabbage with sweet & sour sauce $9.95, Pad Ped $8.95-17.95, Lemon Chicken $8.95, House Curry with kaffir lime leaves, fresh ground lemon grass, peas and coconut milk, chicken, pork or beef $10.95, Mema's Beef Curry $9.95
Adult Beverages: BYOB

Impressions: Authentic Flavors

Mema Thai is situated across the highway from Restaurant Kintaro at the south edge of Kapa'a. As you walk up to the door the first things you'll notice are the rosewood furnishings and art objects that give this restaurant its distinctive and exotic ambiance. From there the intoxicating aromas take off giving hints to the fabulous flavors to be experienced herein. Thai food will never be referred to as boring. This is affordable dining with panache. We recommend it to our friends.

East Coast

Mermaids Café ✓✓✓

4-1384 Kuhio Hwy (Hwy 56)
Kapa'a, HI 96746
808-821-2026
Web: None
Hours: LD 11:00AM-8:45PM
Cards: MC V
Dress: Casual
Style: Healthy Island $

Menu Sampler:

Kids Menu Too

Breakfast:
N/A
Lunch/Dinner:
Ahi Nori Wrap of seared ahi in a 12" green tortilla with rice, cucumber, nori, wasabi cream sauce, pickled ginger, soy sauce $8.95, Tropical Tacos of two corn tortillas filled with ahi cooked in a special sauce, with black beans, salsa fresca, organic lettuce $8.95, Tofu or Chicken Coconut Curry Plate with vegetables and greens cooked with a mild yellow curry in coconut milk, served over rice $9.95, Ahi Cilantro of seared ahi with special homemade cilantro sauce, rice, cucumber and soy sauce wrapped in a green tortilla $8.95, Organic Salad of fresh local greens with a balsamic vinaigrette and garnished with tomato, cucumber, red onion, chevre or feta and walnuts served with focaccia $8.95, with ahi or chicken $10.95, Focaccia Sandwich of avocado, ahi or chicken served on freshly baked focaccia with pesto aioli, tomato, cucumber, organic greens and red onions $8.95, Black Bean Burritos $8.95
Side Orders: Various sauces, trimmings and salsa $.50 to $1.00
Beverages: Thai iced tea, Organic spearmint and lemongrass iced tea, Tropical hibiscus iced tea, Home made lemonade, Tropical hibiscus lemonade $2.00
Adult Beverages: N/A

Impressions:

Funky Walk-up

We first heard about Mermaids from a surfer dude we picked up hitchhiking. He told us about a place in Kapa'a that had the best ahi nori wrap on the planet. Not easily convinced we marched up to their window and ordered one. It didn't take more than a couple bites for us to agree that he was absolutely right! If you want to escape the usual give Mermaids a try. It doesn't look like much, but the staff works magic in the tiny kitchen. Fresh organic ingredients appear frequently as vegetarians and vegans are catered to. Sit on the stools alongside the building if it's hot out front. The fresh ocean breeze will cool you off like air-conditioning.

Kauai Dining

North Shore

Neide's Salsa & Samba ✓
Hanalei Center
5-5161 Kuhio Hwy (Hwy 56)
Hanalei, HI 96714
808-826-1851

Web:	None
Hours:	L 11:30 AM-2:30 PM D 5:00 PM-Closing
Cards:	MC V
Dress:	Casual
Style:	Brazilian/Mexican $

Menu Sampler:

Kids Menu Too

Breakfast:
N/A
Lunch/Dinner:
Mexican Dishes: Macho Burrito with refried beans, cheese and onions, choice of shredded beef, chicken, pork or veggies, topped with ranchera sauce, melted cheese, sour cream and black olives $8.95, Huevos Ranchera of two eggs sunny side up on a crisp, flat corn tortilla with refried beans, ranchera sauce, sour cream and black olives, served with Spanish rice and flour tortilla $8.95, Nachos with black olives $4.50
Brazilian Dishes: Panqueca of a crepe with pumpkin stuffing and fresh vegetables smothered in Neide's own special sauce with melted cheese and fresh vegetables & cheese served with Brazilian rice $9.95, Ensopado of chicken and fresh vegetables baked with a special Brazilian sauce served with Brazilian rice and black beans $10.95, Bife Acebolado tender, juicy beef steak smothered in fresh Maui onions served with Brazilian rice and black beans $15.95
A La Carte: Taco with choice of meats or veggie $3.50, Enchilada with choice of meats or veggie $3.50, Cheese Quesadilla $4.00, add choice of meats $2.00
Adult Beverages: Beer/Wine/Cocktails

Impressions:

Lite Tastes

Neide's Salsa & Samba is located in the back of the Hanalei Center and shares a courtyard dining area with Bar Acuda. If it rains take a seat in the indoor dining room set with wooden tables and chairs. Since they opened in 1998 Neide's has developed a loyal following of locals and visitors who enjoy their large servings of Mexican and Brazilian dishes. For those new to Brazilian cuisine it is long on meat courses and comes in sizeable portions. All of the dishes served at Neide's are mildly seasoned in the Brazilian tradition. Expect gentle, interesting flavors.

East Coast

Norberto's El Café ✓

4-1373 Kuhio Hwy (Hwy 56)
Kapa'a, HI 96746
808-822-3362
Web: None
Hours: D 5:00 PM-9:00 PM XSu
Cards: AE DIS MC V
Dress: Casual
Style: Mexican $$

Menu Sampler:

Kids Menu Too

Breakfast/Lunch:
N/A

Dinner:
All dinners are served with soup, Spanish rice, refried beans, corn chips and plenty of hot Mexican salsa. Burrito Ranchero of ground beef $15.45, Beef Tostada-Enchilada Combination made with a crispy corn tortilla with seasoned beef, refried beans, cheddar cheese, lettuce, Spanish enchilada sauce and tomatoes served with one jack and cheddar cheese enchilada $15.45, Rellenos Tampico select green chile stuffed with natural Monterey Jack cheese dipped in whipped egg and sautéed to a golden brown, with Spanish sauce and cheese and a tasty cheese enchilada $17.95, Mex-Mix Plate with a chicken chimichanga, a chicken taquito, and a cheese enchilada with guacamole $17.95. A la carte items range from a $5.25 Taco, $8.95 for a Nachos Supreme, $9.45 for a Burrito Outrageous, to $14.45 for a Rellenos Plate.
Dessert: Hula Pie $3.50, Rum Cake $3.50, Ice Cream $2.50
Adult Beverages: Beer/Wine/Cocktails – Corkage Fee $5.00

Impressions:

Old Mexico

Norberto's has been around Kapa'a Town so long we sometimes wonder which came first, the restaurant or the building. The menu is traditional zesty Mexican with some notable twists. First, in order to meet heart-healthy standards, no lard or animal fat is used. Then, as a concession to the regular clientele, many dishes may be requested vegetarian. In fact, one of their house favorites is an enchilada stuffed with eggplant rather than meat. For a Hawaiian touch the restaurant also features homegrown taro leaf enchiladas. Fish specials are offered when they're available. The house cantina serves authentic Margaritas by the glass or pitcher.

East Coast

Ono Family Restaurant ✓✓

4-1292 Kuhio Hwy (Hwy 56)
Kapa'a, HI 96746
808-822-1710
Web: None
Hours: B 7:00 AM-1:00 PM
L 11:00 AM-2:00 PM
Cards: AE DC JCB MC V
Dress: Casual
Style: American/Island $

Menu Sampler:

Kids Menu Too

Breakfast:
All meals with toast have a choice of branola or sourdough or add an English muffin for $.25, Eggs & Hash corned beef hash with two poached eggs, toast, side of hollandaise and a slice of papaya $7.75, Eggs Canterbury poached eggs, ham, turkey, jack cheese, tomato, hollandaise sauce and mushrooms on English muffin with a slice of papaya $8.95. Three-Egg Omelets include your choice of fillings and choice of hash browns, rice, fried rice or toast $6.25-$8.75, Tropical Stack with bananas, macadamia nuts, coconut and whipped cream $6.50
Lunch:
Farmer's Sandwich of turkey, ham, jack cheese, lettuce, tomato and mayonnaise on Branola bread with French fries and soup $8.25, Chicken Breast Plate served with rice or fries and choice of teriyaki or BBQ sauce and soup or salad $8.95, Saimin local noodle soup topped with wonbok, carrots, green onions and half hard-boiled egg, small $4.25, large $6.25, Burgers served with fries or salad $6.20 to $8.20, Oriental Chicken Salad stir-fried chicken breast on greens $8.25, Fresh Fish Plate/Sandwich ono or ahi with rice or fries and soup or salad $8.20
Dessert: Coconut or Macadamia Nut Custard Homemade Pie $3.95/slice.
Adult Beverages: BYOB with verifiable ID
Dinner:
N/A

Impressions:

Extensive Menu

Kapa'a may have changed around it but this plantation-era restaurant remains a great breakfast and lunch choice. Their lengthy menu features two pages of egg dishes alone containing local favorites like homemade chorizo, lup cheong, and kim chee. Although steamed rice or potatoes are available with most dishes, we think their fried rice is the big hit. This daytime hangout is full of aloha and is a "must try" for the adventurous traveler. Once again be sure to save room for pie.

East Coast

Pacific Island Bistro ✓✓✓

Kauai Village Shopping Center
4-831 Kuhio Hwy (Hwy 56)
Kapa'a, HI 96746
808-822-0092
www.kauaibistro.com
Hours: L 10:30 AM-3:00 PM XTh
D 4:00 PM-9:30 PM Th
D 3:00 PM-9:30 PM Fr-We
Cards: AE DIS JCB MC V
Dress: Casual
Style: Asian Pacific $$

Menu Sampler:

Breakfast:
N/A
Lunch:
Kalua Pull Pork Sandwich with waffle fries $10.95, Mahi Mahi Sandwich pan fried with Asian pesto, waffle fries $9.95, Bistro Shrimp Omelet with shrimp, tomato, onion, bean sprout, chef's special gravy, jasmine rice $9.95
Lunch and Dinner:
Appetizer: Soft Shell Crab Tempura with coconut wasabi aioli $9.95, Lettuce Taco with Minced Pork in hoisin mango sauce $7.95, Bistro Crab Cake $9.95
Entrées: Pan Seared Opakapaka in mango Thai curry, garlic mash potato with diced tomato and wild mushroom $18.95, Pork Tenderloin dusted in five spices flour, pan fried with green peppercorn, brandy and a light blue cheese cream sauce with garlic mashed potato $16.95, Pacific Island Curry $12.95
Ala Carte: Choose One: Seafood Combination $13.95, Sea Bass Fillet $13.95, Black Tiger Shrimp $11.95, Scallop $12.95, Chicken, Beef or Pork $9.95, Vegetable, Eggplant or Tofu $8.95. Sauce: Hot Mongolian, Red Curry, Coconut Cream, Ginger Garlic, Broccoli Oyster, Garlic Black Bean and Garlic Wine
Adult Beverages: Beer/Wine/Cocktails – Corkage Fee $12.00

Impressions: Innovative Chinese

We love following the restaurant scene. Things tend to be so predictable. Once a location becomes a restaurant spot, it's always a restaurant spot. Here is a classic example. This is the former home of one of our favorite Chinese dining spots on the Coconut Coast. Now, the same owners have reinvented themselves revealing complexity found only in more upscale establishments. Don't let the multicenter location concern you. This Asian fusion experience will satisfy discerning tastes.

West Side

Pacific Pizza & Deli ✓
9852 Kaumualii Hwy (Hwy 50)
Waimea, HI 96796
808-338-1020
Web: None
Hours: LD 11:00 AM-9:00 PM XSu
Cards: DIS MC V
Dress: Casual
Style: Italian $

Menu Sampler:

Breakfast:
N/A
Lunch/Dinner:
Pizzas & Calzones:
Pacific Pepperoni - Small $8.25, Medium $14.95, Large $18.25, Calzone $6.00
Surfa Deluxe - pesto sauce, Canadian bacon, shrimp, faux crab and pineapple - Small $9.25, Medium $15.25, Large $20.25, Calzone $6.50
Lomi Lomi - cheeses, fresh tomatoes, diced salmon, diced onions and green onions - Small $9.25, Medium $15.25, Large $20.25, Calzone $6.75
Hapa Haole - pesto sauce, cheeses, sun-dried tomatoes, mushrooms, zucchini, olives, Canadian bacon and pineapple - Small $9.25, Medium $15.25, Large $20.25, Calzone $6.75
Portuguese - house Portuguese sausage, onions, olives and more - Small $8.95, Medium $14.95, Large $19.50, Calzone $6.00
Additional Toppings: Small $.75, Medium $1.45, Large $2.25, Calzone $.50
Cold Wraps: with turkey, chicken, roast beef, pastrami, ham or veggies $5.25, seafood $6.25 in a tomato-basil tortilla with house special dressing
Deli Sandwiches: with choice of meat and bread with fresh toppings $5.25
Sides: House Salad $3.75, Pizza Bread $3.75
Adult Beverages: Beer/Wine/Cocktails

Impressions: Island Pizzeria

Located in a breezy plantation style building alongside Wrangler's Steakhouse you'll find Pacific Pizza & Deli. High ceilings, wood floors and antiques are a proper setting for the quality pizza and calzone coming out of the kitchen. The yeasty crust is puffy on the edges while thin and crispy in the center, even with all the toppings. Sometimes we find it difficult to procure good Italian sausage in the islands, but theirs' has that tantalizing taste of fennel. A small pizza will feed two people generously making this an affordable choice for casual dining.

South Shore

Additional Location

Pizzetta ✓✓
5408 Koloa Road
Koloa, HI 96756
808-742-8881
www.pizzettarestaurant.com
Hours: LD 11:00 AM-9:30 PM
Cards: MC V
Dress: Casual
Style: Italian $$

4-1387 Kuhio Hwy
Kapa'a, HI 96746
808-823-8882

Menu Sampler:

Kids Menu Too

Breakfast:
N/A
Lunch:
Sandwiches & Pasta: Veneto of blackened chicken, Cajun dressing, mozzarella cheese, lettuce & tomato w/pasta salad $7.95, Homemade Meatball oven baked w/marinara, roasted garlic cream sauce & mozzarella, open-faced w/pasta salad $6.95, Pasta Lunch Special penne w/choice of sauce, house salad & bread $8.95
Pizza: Traditional or Gourmet, Thin Crust or Regular. Medium $16.95-$17.95, Large $19.95-$22.95, additional toppings add $2.25 each
Dinner:
Antipasti, Salads & Sides: Hot Crab & Artichoke Dip with Crostini $9.95, Garlic Bread Sticks with marinara sauce $5.95, Caesar Salad $4.95-$7.95
Entrées: Penne Rossa w/ Italian Sausage $15.95, Chicken Marsala w/penne or garlic mashed potatoes $16.95, Eggplant Parmesan w/pasta or garlic mashed potatoes $13.95, Lasagne $13.95, Fettuccini Lucia $15.95, Spaghetti with Meatballs $12.95, Fettuccini Quattro Formaggio $11.95, Penne Pesto $11.95
Pizza: Handmade herb crust thin or regular, medium or large $13.95-$22.95, Pizza by the Slice $2.95-$3.70 served from 11:00 AM to 6:00 PM
Daily Specials: BBQ Pork Ribs $15.95, Grilled Ono with fruit salsa $15.95, Grilled Ono Caesar Salad $15.95, Shrimp Fettuccini $17.95 no carb add $2.95
Adult Beverages: Beer/Wine/Cocktails – Corkage Fee $12.00

Impressions:

Italian Tavern

After several days of fine dining you might desire something more casual before the next extravaganza. That is where Pizzetta comes in. Here you will find pizza parlor favorites served in a convivial family atmosphere. This happening spot is not just for visitors though as local people like to gather here for happy hour and revelry late into the evening. If you're up on the East Coast checkout the Kapa'a location. Based on the customer comings and goings they're getting it done also.

South Shore

Plantation Gardens ✓✓✓

Kiahuna Plantation Resort
2253 Poipu Road
Koloa, HI 96756
808-742-2216
www.pgrestaurant.com
Hours: D 5:30 PM-9:00PM
Cards: AE DC MC V
Dress: Resort Casual
Style: Pacific Rim $$$

Menu Sampler:

Kids Menu Too

Breakfast/Lunch:
N/A
Dinner:
Pupus: Spicy Ahi Poke w/Maui onions, scallions, purple sweet potato chips and sesame-sweet soy vinaigrette 11.95, Roasted Duck Spring Rolls, sweet soy sauce 9.95, Thai Beef Lettuce Wrap, roasted peanuts, chilies, papaya salsa 10.95
Salads: Caesar Salad with macadamia nut-basil croutons 8.95, Spinach & Arugula Salad with Kauai orange segments, red onions, balsamic basil vinaigrette 9.95, Kamuela Tomato Salad with arugula, shaved red onion, Kalamata olives, Roquefort cheese and Thai basil-lemon vinaigrette 10.95
Entrées: Kiawe Grilled Ahi, rice, sautéed local baby spinach, tropical fruit and avocado salsa with kaffir lime cream sauce 26.95, Garden Isle Bouillabaisse of local fish, prawns, bay scallops, mussels, roasted potatoes, grilled crostini and Kamuela tomato-saffron broth 25.95, Baby Back Pork Ribs braised in house made barbecue sauce, roasted garlic mashed potatoes and local seasonal vegetables 22.95, Kiawe Grilled New York Strip Steak, goat cheese potato gratin, braised broccolini, caramelized Maui onion and shiitake mushroom jus 26.95, Roasted Half Chicken with roasted garlic-wasabi mashed potatoes, braised baby bok choy and house made ponzu sauce 19.95
Desserts: Coconut Crème Brulee 6.95, Local Lilikoi Cheesecake 6.95
Adult Beverages: Beer/Wine/Cocktails – Corkage Fee 10.00

Impressions:

Genteel Ambiance

This historic Old Hawaii estate with its high ceilings, cherry floors, koa trim and hand-painted murals was called home by the manager of the Kiahuna Plantation. Today it's a luxurious open-air dining venue serving award-winning Pacific Rim cuisine with occasional Mediterranean twists. Whether your party prefers drinks and pupus in the lounge or dinner on the veranda, a first-class experience awaits.

South Shore

Poipu Bay Clubhouse and Yum Cha ✓✓

Grand Hyatt Golf Club
2250 Ainako Road
Koloa, HI 96756
808-742-1515
www.kauai.hyatt.com

Hours: B 7:00 AM-10:30 AM Mo-Sa
L 10:30 AM-2:30 PM
BL 7:00 AM-2:30 PM Su
D 5:30 PM-9:30 PM Tu-Sa
Cards: AE DC DIS JCB MC V
Dress: Casual
Style: BL American/Island - D Asian Fusion $$

Menu Sampler: Kids Menu Too

Breakfast:
Poipu Delight - trio of pancakes with blueberries, bananas and mango $12, Broke Da Mouth! - three egg frittata w/Portuguese sausage, provolone cheese, tomatoes, green onion & fried rice $12, Da Kamaaina - local favorite $12
Lunch:
Pacific Rim Chicken Salad in won ton cup with Chinese mustard vinaigrette $15, Portuguese Bean Soup $6, Poipu Bay's Fish & Chips with garlic fries and coleslaw $16, Crab Cake Sandwich on Hawaiian Bread with slaw $17
Dinner:
Yum Cha Restaurant Appetizers: Wok Seared Edamame with garlic hoisin sauce $7, Lettuce Wraps, roasted chicken, glass noodles, cashews $10
Soups & Salads: Tom Yum Soup $9/$18, Green Papaya Salad $10
Large Plates: Yum Cha Fried Rice, vegetables, eggs $10, Szechuan Sautéed Prime Beef, green chilies, ginger $21, Mandarin Chicken, orange-soy glaze $16, Fried Soba Noodles $10, Steamed Hawaiian Snapper, vegetables, tofu $24
Happy Endings: Tempura Fried Banana with macadamia nut ice cream $5
Adult Beverages: Beer/Wine/Cocktails – Corkage Fee $25

Impressions: Clubhouse Plus

Those who remember grabbing a cup of coffee and a roll before teeing off will appreciate this place more than most. Clubhouse dining has come of age in this gracious room overlooking the Hyatt course. The menu offers sophistication in line with the mega-facility. Preparations lean toward complex where traditional dishes and exotic ingredients are tweaked with island techniques. Note that the cuisine style makes a big change to Asian Fusion at dinner. It sounds intriguing.

South Shore

Poipu Beach Broiler ✓✓✓

1941 Poipu Road
Koloa, HI 96756
808-742-6433
www.pbbroiler.com
Hours: L 11:30 AM-3:00 PM
Lite Menu 3:00 PM-5:00 PM
D 5:00 PM-10:00 PM
Cards: AE DC DIS MC V
Dress: Resort Casual
Style: Island/Pacific Rim $$

Menu Sampler:

Kids Menu Too

Breakfast:
N/A
Lunch:
Appetizers: Baby Back Ribs with bourbon-pineapple bbq sauce $10, Island Style Hot Wings $10, Vegetable Spring Rolls $8, Pan Seared Ahi Sashimi, peppercorn dusted & served with spicy mustard & Indonesian sweet soy $13
Salads: Salad Bar $8, Caesar Salad with lemon anchovy vinaigrette $9
Main Courses: Fish & Chips w/fries & lemon remoulade sauce $11, Teriyaki Chicken Sandwich with caramelized pineapple $9, Fresh Ahi Tuna Sandwich $10, Daily Plate Lunch $9, French Dip Sandwich $10, Fish Tacos $12
Dinner:
Appetizers: Lobster & Crab Ravioli $12, Sautéed Mushrooms $9
Entrées: Macadamia Nut Crusted Local Island Fish with rice and Kahana Royale beurre blanc $21, Blackened "Daily Fish" with Madame Pele's heat and sweet mango compote $26, Southwestern Spiced Ahi with brandied lobster sauce $26, Baby Back Pork Ribs w/garlic whipped potato, house made bourbon & pineapple bbq sauce $23, Grilled Top Sirloin Steak, garlic whipped potatoes, compound butter $23, Lobster & Crab Ravioli, tomato pesto cream $21
Desserts: Chocolate Mousse $6, Luau Dream Sorbet $5
Adult Beverages: Beer/Wine/Cocktails – Corkage Fee $10

Impressions:

Casual Hideaway

This used to be The House Of Seafood. A few years back new owners appeared and took the place down to the bare walls. Not only did the atmosphere improve but so did the menu. Chef Brant Hunt prepares exciting dishes with layers upon layers of flavor. His gift is taking something common and adding spins to come up with results that far exceed the sum of the parts. With that said fish still rules!

West Side

Pomodoro Restaurant ✓✓✓

Rainbow Plaza
2-2514 Kaumualii Hwy (Hwy 50)
Kalaheo, HI 96741
808-332-5945
Web: None
Hours: D 5:30 PM-9:30 PM XSu
Cards: MC V
Dress: Resort Casual
Style: Classic Italian $$

Menu Sampler: Kids Menu Too

Breakfast/Lunch:
N/A
Dinner:
All dinners include the house home baked foccacia.
Antipasti & Zuppe: Calamari Fritti $13.50, Mozzarella Marinara $9.50, Prosciutto & Melon (or seasonal fruit) $10.50, Minestrone alla Pomodoro $4.50
Insalate: Caesar $8.95, Mixed Greens with light balsamic vinaigrette $7.95
Pasta: Spaghetti Bolognese or Marinara Sauce $14.95, w/Meatballs or Italian Sausage $17.95, Tortellini alla Panna $17.95, Manicotti filled with a blend of cheeses $16.95, Lasagne (House Special) with Italian sausage and choice beef $17.95, Linguini White or Red Clam Sauce $19.95, Fettuccine Alfredo $15.95, Ravioli Marinara or Bolognese $16.95, w/Meatballs or Italian Sausage $18.95
Specialties: All dishes are served with farfelle pasta with seasonal vegetables. Veal Pizzaiola with roasted peppers and onions in house special wine sauce $24.95, Chicken Saltimbocca $22.95, Eggplant Parmigiana $21.95, Scampi $24.95, Veal Scaloppini Al Marsala $24.95, Scampi in a fresh garlic, caper and wine sauce $24.95, Veal Piccata $24.95, Calamari Steak Parmigiana $21.95
Desserts: Assorted Italian desserts daily $8.00
Beverages: Espresso $2.75, Cappuccino $3.25, Café Latte $3.50
Adult Beverages: Beer/Wine/Cocktails – Corkage Fee $15.00

Impressions: Worth Driving

This intimate bistro-style establishment can be found on the second floor of the Rainbow Plaza on the north side of Kalaheo. After cocktails dinner begins with the house wait staff delivering the authentic Italian cuisine this family operated dining room is known for. Afterwards there's a wonderful dessert tray to tempt everyone. The combination of quality and reasonable prices seen here make the short drive over from Poipu Beach well worthwhile. Reservations are advisable.

North Shore

Postcards Café ✓✓

5-5075A Kuhio Hwy (Hwy 56)
Hanalei, HI 96714
808-826-1191
www.postcardscafe.com
Hours: D 6:00 PM-9:00 PM
Cards: AE MC V
Dress: Casual
Style: Upscale Vegetarian/Seafood $$

Menu Sampler: Kids Menu Too

Breakfast/Lunch:
N/A
Dinner:
First Taste: Hanalei Taro Fritters polenta crusted with pineapple ginger salsa 9.00, Thai Summer Rolls fresh or seared, spicy peanut sauce 9.00, Seafood Rockets wrapped in lumpia, sweet red chili sauce 12.00, Porcini Crusted Scallops sautéed with mushrooms & greens, cashew-date dressing 11.00, Crab Quesadillas black bean and papaya salsa, chipotle chile sour cream 12.00, Caesar Salad with homemade croutons 9.00, Savory Soups 7.00
Entrées: Seafood Sorrento a pasta with fresh fish and shrimp sautéed with onions, mushrooms, tomatoes, bell peppers, Kalamata olives and capers in a garlic-white wine sauce 24.00, Island Fish grilled or blackened, with rice, vegetables and a choice of sauces; honey ginger Dijon, macadamia nut butter or peppered pineapple sage $Market, The Francesca a puttanesca with sun-dried tomatoes, pepperoncini, Kalamata and green olives in a sherry marinara sauce 18.00, with shrimp 24.00, The Shanghai sautéed tofu and crisp vegetables w/ roasted cashews in a tamari ginger sauce over rice pilaf 18.00, with shrimp 24.00, Wasabi Crusted Ahi in a mirin shoyu ginger sauce, rice, veg. 27.00
Desserts: Pineapple Upside Down Cake, coconut sorbet 9.00, Chocolate Silk Pie 7.00, Lilikoi Mousse 7.00, Banana Mac Pie 7.00, Coconut Sorbet 7.00
Adult Beverages: Beer/Wine – Corkage Fee 10.00

Impressions: Healthy Dining

Look for the quaint plantation cottage home of Postcards mauka of the highway as you enter Hanalei. Indoor/outdoor dining is offered in this picturesque village setting. The vegetarian influenced menu is designed around natural and organic ingredients, although fish and shellfish are offered as a nod to Kauai tastes. This little spot seems to attract its fair share of celebrities and loyal patrons, so phone ahead as reservations are recommended. Check the hours - they vary by season.

South Shore

Puka Dog ✓

Poipu Shopping Village
2360 Kiahuna Plantation Drive
Koloa, HI 96756
808-979-2405
www.pukadog.com
Hours: LD 11:00 AM-6:00 PM
Cards: None
Dress: Casual
Style: Hawaiian Style Hot Dogs $

Menu Sampler:

Breakfast:
N/A
Lunch/Dinner:
Puka Dog: Starts with a bun toasted in an unusual way - up through the middle! Then, either a Polish or Veggie Dog is inserted into the roll, a mild, spicy or hot sauce is added before a mango, pineapple, papaya, coconut, banana or star fruit tropical relish is applied. Three kinds of ketchup are available for your selection: yellow, Dijon or lilikoi sweet. This large sandwich is all you'll need for $5.95.
Sides: A bag of Maui Chips $1.00, Fresh Squeezed Lemonade $2.00
Adult Beverages: N/A

Impressions:

Novelty Stop

Let's start at the beginning. In Hawaiian the word "puka" means "hole". Here at Puka Dog the puka refers to the hole that is punched into the sandwich roll when it is skewered onto the toaster. Toasting from the inside seals the puka so sauces, relishes, and garnishes can be safely added alongside the dog. This novel grilling approach allows for the unique combination of flavors that can be enjoyed while you stroll about Poipu Shopping Village. Customers have their choice of quality dogs and sauces to match their personality. We recommend including one of the tropical relishes for a touch of Hawaii. Remember the fresh squeezed lemonade!

Restaurant Kintaro ✓✓✓
4370 Kuhio Hwy (Hwy 56)
Kapa'a, HI 96746
808-822-3341
Web: None
Hours: D 5:30 PM-9:00 PM XSu
Cards: AE DC DIS JCB MC V
Dress: Resort Casual
Style: Japanese $$

Menu Sampler:

Breakfast/Lunch:
N/A
Dinner:
Sushi: Maki Sushi (cut rolls) and Temaki Sushi (hand rolls) Kilauea Roll slightly smoked salmon, tuna (ahi), avocado & Maui onions $9.00/half roll $5.50, Shrimp Tempura Roll with cucumber, radish sprouts & tobiko rolled in seasoned rice & seaweed $10.00 with unagi $12.95, Chirashi-Sushi $13.95
Appetizers: Lemon Buttered Mussels in shell (4 pcs) $3.95, Gyoza fried dumpling (5 pcs) $5.50, Crispy Won Ton from owner's factory (8 pcs) $3.50
Dinners: Served with chilled buckwheat noodles and sauce, miso soup, rice, Japanese pickles and tea. Tempura Combination of local fish, shrimp and a variety of fresh vegetables $13.95, Yakitori chicken with onion, bell pepper, teriyaki sauce and salad $13.50, Dinner Special combinations $15.95-$16.95
Teppan Yaki: Chef is entertaining as he prepares the meal on a tableside grill. Dinners are served with miso soup or salad, shellfish, seafood, mushroom and fresh island vegetables prepared teppan style. Oysters sautéed with olive oil $15.95, Filet Mignon $24.95, Hibachi Shrimp $18.95, Island Chicken Teriyaki $15.95, Steak Teriyaki $23.95, Fresh Island Fish with Scallops $Market Price
Nabe Mono: One pot chafing dish with seafood and vegetables $10.95-$14.95, Sukiyaki Dinner in a sweet soy sauce with miso soup and seafood salad $15.95
Adult Beverages: Beer/Wine/Cocktails – Corkage Fee $9.00-$12.00

Impressions: Everything Japanese

Even though Restaurant Kintaro is much larger inside than it looks, you need to determine the Japanese dining style you prefer before making reservations. This rambling establishment offers their patrons sushi bar, teppanyaki grill, teishoku table and tatami room seating. If we were only allowed one recommendation on Kauai for experiencing Japanese cuisine this would be it. As a waiting customer once said to us, "Best sukiyaki I ever had, and I eat it a lot". Always call ahead.

South Shore

Roy's Poipu Bar & Grill ✓✓✓✓

Poipu Shopping Village
2360 Kiahuna Plantation Drive
Koloa, HI 96756
808-742-5000
www.roysrestaurant.com
Hours: D 5:30 PM-9:30 PM
Cards: AE DC JCB MC V
Dress: Resort Casual
Style: Hawaiian Fusion $$$

Menu Sampler: Kids Menu Too

Breakfast/Lunch:
N/A
Dinner:
Appetizers: Roy's Original Blackened Island Ahi, spicy hot mustard soy butter sauce $14.50/$30.50, Minted Chicken & Basil Spring Rolls w/sweet chili peanut vinaigrette $10.00, Shrimp & Asparagus Crepes with chevre, pesto butter and rosemary demi-glace $14.50, 'Canoe For Two' appetizer $28.00, Granny Smith Apple and Gorgonzola Salad w/candied walnuts & a sesame miso vinaigrette $10.00, Assorted Nigiri Sushi $15.50, Kiyo's Inside Out Maki Roll $15.50
Entrées: Roy's Classic Macadamia Nut Opah with lobster butter sauce $32.50, Jade Pesto Steamed Hawaiian King Moi Chinese style sizzling ginger peanut oil $36.50, Teriyaki Grilled Salmon cucumber namasu, citrus ponzu sauce $13.00 and $28.50, Herb Grilled White Shrimp pecorino romano, roasted garlic lemon caper scampi sauce $28.50, Herb Grilled Portobello Mushroom charred tomato, caramelized onions & ko chu jang beurre blanc $15.00 Slow Braised Beef Short Ribs creamy gratin potatoes, veal demi glace & lomi tomatoes $28.50, Rustic Charred 10oz Ribeye Steak Maui onion, gremolata & horseradish cream $33.50, Roy's "Classic Trio" Blackened Ahi, Hibachi Salmon & Miso Butterfish $34.50
Adult Beverages: Beer/Wine/Cocktails – Corkage Fee $18.00

Impressions: Expect Excellence

Chef Roy Yamaguchi was one of the founding members of the Hawaii Regional Cuisine movement that began in the late 1980's to promote the use of fresh local produce, fish, and meats in island cooking. His style of culinary fusion launched Roy's Restaurants into the global marketplace of fine dining. Every dish offered at this casual but upscale eatery uses herbs and spices from diverse cuisines for a real flavor explosion! Listen for the daily specials and check out the dessert tray. Roy's Poipu has expanded into additional space, but reservations are still a must.

hore

Saffron ✓✓✓

Pali Ke Kua Condos
5300 Ka Haku Road
Princeville, HI 96722
808-826-6225
www.saffron-hawaii.com
Hours: D 6:00 PM-9:00 PM
Cards: MC V
Dress: Resort Casual
Style: Mediterranean $$$

Menu Sampler: Small Plates Too

Breakfast/Lunch:
N/A
Dinner:
La España: Sautéed Mushrooms 13, Carpaccio with Tenderloin 14, with ahi 16, Garlic Lime Prawns 17, Tortilla Española Spanish style potato frittata 13, Paella with seafood, chicken, chorizo 15/27, Almond-Saffron Crusted Ahi, vegetables, garlic potatoes 33, Grilled Rack of Lamb, cranberry 17, Crusted Ahi 33,
La Italia: Shrimp, Black Olive, Feta & Roasted Red Peppers Pizzeta 16/21, Margarita Pizzeta 14/19, Pepperoni Pizzeta 14/17, Caesar Salad 12, Tomato Mozzarella Salad with Buffalo mozzarella, tomato, basil 9, Mushroom Ravioli with creamy sun dried tomato and basil sauce, Assiago & Parmesan cheese 20, Penne Alfredo 18, Ossobucco 34, Spaghetti Marinara with Parmesan 18
La Grecia: Philo Wrapped Baked Brie, blueberry sauce 13, Humus & Grilled Vegetables, flat bread & tzaski 12, Betty Salad of shrimp, goat cheese, cucumbers, tomatoes & spicy vinaigrette 14, Grilled Chicken with honey glaze and orzo salad 24, Beef Tenderloin with Date Demiglaze with roasted potatoes, asparagus and feta cheese, date and red wine demiglaze 35, Rack of Lamb with roasted garlic, roasted potatoes, mushroom demiglaze with asparagus 39
Dessert: Flan 10, Tiramisu 9, Baklava 8, Lava Chocolate Cake 8, Apple Tart 8
Adult Beverages: Beer/Wine Cellar/Cocktails – Corkage Fee 8-10

Impressions: Evening's Retreat

North Shore diners have a new option that deserves a good look. Out in a condo complex near the St. Regis Hotel you'll find an evening oasis that goes by the name of Saffron. Their menu revolves around three ever popular Mediterranean cuisines with patrons choosing from Spanish, Italian, and Greek specialties. It's perfect for grazers and tapas dining with lite bites offered from all of the above. Unlike the fusion approach each different regional style is kept true to its origin.

East Coast

Scotty's Beachside BBQ

4-1546 Kuhio Hwy (Hwy 56)
Kapa'a, HI 96746
808-823-8480
www.scottysbbq.com
Hours: 11:00AM-9:00PM XMo
Cards: AE DIS JCB MC V
Dress: Casual
Style: American $$

Menu Sampler:

Kids Menu Too

Breakfast:
N/A

Lunch:
Sandwiches: All come w/choice of fries, baked beans, cole slaw, or mac salad. Pulled Pork on a hoagie $10.99, Beef Brisket (1/3#) $10.99, Smoked Breast of Chicken $10.99, Mahi-Mahi $11.99, Open Face Sandwich Sampler $12.49, All American Burger w/fries $10.99, Veggie Patty Burger w/fries $11.99
Lunch Favorites: Half-Rack Ribs & Beans $16.99, Fish and Chips $16.99

Dinner:
Appetizers: 1/3 Rack of Ribs $12.50, Pulled Pork Nachos $12.99, Grilled Shrimp $12.99, Fried Coconut Shrimp $14.49, Potato Skins, pulled pork $12.99
Salads: Spinach Salad $11.99, Caesar Salad $11.99, Garden Salad $10.99
Entrées: All served with baked beans, fries and choice of cornbread or garlic bread. Half Rack Ribs $22.99, Full Rack Ribs $30.99, Smoked Pork, Beef Brisket or Smoked Chicken $21.99, BBQ Sampler for one $23.99, for two $44.99, Grilled Shrimp Dinner $24.99, Fish & Chips, fries $16.99, Mahi $Mkt
Desserts: Chocolate Coma Cake $11.50, Chocolate Lava Eruption $8.75, Make Your Own S'Mores $11.99 for Two, Coconut Cream Pie $7.25, Puffasada $9.75
Adult Beverages: Beer/Wine/Cocktails – Corkage Fee $10.00

Impressions:

Slow Smoker

Have you ever noticed that BBQ is a lot like pizza? Everywhere you go it's a bit different but always good. That's the tale here in Kapa'a where smoke and sauce rule the pit instead of flame. Of course, this wouldn't be Kauai without a unique spin so the cook uses both kiawe and hickory to create flavors. The meat lingers in the plume for hours getting a full dose of natural essence while retaining most of the moisture. All this doesn't come cheap, but BBQ fans will love the results. If you have someone in your party with different druthers they can by-pass these riches and enjoy alternative selections without compromise. Be creative parking.

West Side

Shrimp Station Restaurant ✓
9652 Kaumualii Hwy (Hwy 50)
Waimea, HI 96796
808-338-1242
www.shrimpstation.com
Hours: LD 11:00 AM-5:00 PM
Cards: MC V
Dress: Casual
Style: Gourmet Shrimp $$

Menu Sampler: Small Plates/Kids

Breakfast:
N/A
Lunch/Dinner:
Shrimp Tacos two grande flour tortillas filled with sautéed shrimp, fresh veggies and Sid's fresh salsa $12.00, Shrimp Cocktail $4.75, Beer Battered Shrimp dipped in a batter made from ale and fried served with fries and papaya ginger tartar sauce $11.00, Coconut Shrimp dipped in a secret batter, coconut flakes and fried, served with fries and papaya ginger tartar sauce $11.00
Plates: Each comes with a choice of boiled red potatoes or steamed white rice. Got Garlic? (Shrimp Scampi) sautéed in garlic, olive oil and a white wine sauce $11.00, Thai Shrimp (Spicy House Specialty) sautéed in olive oil, fresh basil, white wine & Sid's famous salsa $12.00, Cajun Shrimp sautéed in olive oil, white wine & Sid's classic creamy Cajun sauce $11.00, Sweet Chile Garlic Shrimp, olive oil, garlic, white wine & glazed w/sweet chile sauce $12.00
Shrimp: Served with papaya ginger tartar sauce and French fries. Coconut Shrimp $11.00, Beer Battered Shrimp in a batter made from ale $11.00, Shrimp Tacos (2) w/fresh veggies $12.00, Shrimp Burger w/papaya ginger tartar $8.00
Sides & Miscellaneous: Shrimp Cocktail $4.75, Hot Dog $3.75, Fries $1.75, Chips & Salsa $2.75, Soda & Bottled Water $1.00, Juice & Tea $1.50
Adult Beverages: BYOB

Impressions: Roadside Stand

After sampling the shrimp stands on Oahu's North Shore we often questioned why similar establishments hadn't popped up on any of the other islands. Well we obviously weren't the only ones with that thought. Here on the west side of Kauai, road-trippers will find a little eatery serving all the usual shrimp wagon specialties. This is picnic dining where you place your order at the window and find yourself a seat in the shade. Portions are ample and can be shared if you're looking for a snack. Facilities are available for clean-up before and after eating.

Lihue

Sushi Bushido ✓✓✓
~~Anchor Cove Shopping Center~~
~~3416 Rice Street~~
~~Lihue, HI 96766~~
~~808-632-0664~~ 808-822-0664
4504 Kukui St. Kapa'a (in the Dragon Bldg.)
Web: None
Hours: D 5:00 PM-10:00 PM
Cards: AE DC DIS MC V
Dress: Casual
Style: Japanese/Sushi $$

Menu Sampler:

Small Plates Too

Breakfast/Lunch:
N/A
Dinner:
Nigiri: Maguro $8.00, Hamachi $8.00, Tako $6.00, Ika $6.00, Mirugai $8.00, Ebi $5.00, Amaebi $9.00, Tamago $6.00, Unagi $8.00, Tobiko $6.00, Uni $9.00
Sushi Rolls & Hand Rolls: Tuna Roll $6.95, Cucumber Roll $5.00, Spicy Tuna $8.95, Salmon Skin Roll $8.95, Philly Roll $8.95, Garden Roll $6.95
Specialty Rolls: Lava Roll $12.95, Bushido Roll $12.95, Aloha Roll $10.95, Crackling Shrimp $10.95, Kauai Roll $10.95, Bushido Rainbow Roll $12.95
Lunch Specials: Spicy Chicken $8.95, Chicken Katsu $8.95, Grilled Teriyaki Salmon $13.95, Shrimp and Vegetable Tempura $10.95, Teriyaki Chicken $8.95, Kalua Pork with Lomi Lomi Salmon $10.95 all with rice and tsukemono
From The Kitchen: Shrimp, Fresh Fish or Soft Shell Crab Tempura $13.95, Bushido Spears $12.95, Boss's Steak $20.95, Sensei's Short Ribs $17.95, Spicy Seafood Combo $18.95, Sautéed Oysters $12.95, Haha Wings (hot!) $6.95
Specialty Salads: Bushido Salad $10.95, Sake Salad $10.95, House Salad $8.95
Side Dishes: Tsukemono Salad $3.50, Miso Soup $2.50, Edamame $2.50
Adult Beverages: Beer/Wine/Cocktails – Corkage Fee Varies

Impressions:

Variety & Quality

Anchor Cove Shopping Plaza is a worthwhile visitor stop all by itself. Thanks to its proximity to the cruise ship dock foot traffic has increased immensely. Along with all the other improvements came a truly excellent Hawaii-style sushi house known as Sushi Bushido. This is contemporary sushi with a local dining spin. A lengthy menu is offered with prices that shouldn't scare anyone. Diners will find accommodating service and a view that's hard to beat. Non-sushi guests should enjoy this oceanfront venue as well. There's something here to please everyone.

East Coast

The Bull Shed ✓✓

4-796 Kuhio Hwy (Hwy 56)
Kapa'a, HI 96746
808-822-3791
www.bullshedrestaurant.com
Hours: D 5:30 PM-9:15 PM
Cards: AE DC DIS MC V
Dress: Casual
Style: American/Seafood $$

Menu Sampler:

Kids Menu Too

Breakfast/Lunch:
N/A
Dinner:
All dinners include steamed rice, bread & butter and a trip to the salad bar. Broiled Shrimp or Teriyaki Broiled Shrimp $15.95, Scallops Bull Shed sea scallops sprinkled with parmesan cheese and baked in white wine sauce with sliced mushrooms $17.95, Prime Rib (house specialty) $23.95, Pork Baby Back Ribs $18.95, Garlic Tenderloin or Tenderloin Filet $20.95, Grilled Teriyaki Chicken $14.95, Garlic Chicken $14.95, Australian Lamb Rack a full rack marinated in an herbal red wine recipe and then broiled $26.95, Teriyaki Beef Kebobs broiled with crisp vegetables $9.95, Teriyaki Top Sirloin marinated in brown sugar, pineapple juice and shoyu sauce $15.95, Black Pepper Tenderloin broiled, smothered in pepper sauce with onion, mushroom and beef au jus mix $20.95, Alaskan King Crab/Grilled Catch of the Day $Market Price
Combinations: Steak & Fresh Fish $18.95, Steak & Broiled Shrimp $20.95, Teriyaki Chicken & Fresh Fish $15.95, Fresh Fish & Shrimp $18.95
Ala Carte: Salad Bar Only $6.95, Baked Potato $1.50, Vegetable Skewer $1.50
For Kids Only: Teriyaki Chicken $7.95, Fresh Fish w/rice and salad bar $8.95
Desserts: homemade ice cream pies and cheesecakes $3.50
Adult Beverages: Beer/Wine/Cocktails – Corkage Fee $11.00

Impressions:

60's Style

This oceanfront restaurant is Kauai's answer to supper club dining. With a salad bar, cocktail lounge, and prime rib in the starring role steak-and-seafood junkies will enjoy a sense of comfort and familiarity. Although décor is not a strong suit the solid menu and friendly service continue to please. On warm evenings try to get a table by the windows for a cooling breeze. Locating the entrance can be an interesting experience for first-time clientele. Look across the highway from the McDonald's at Waipouli Town Center and take the driveway down to the beach.

East Coast

The Eggbert's ✓✓

Coconut Marketplace
4-484 Kuhio Hwy (Hwy 56)
Kapa'a, HI 96746
808-822-3787
Web: None
Hours: B 7:00 AM-3:00 PM
L 11:00 AM-3:00 PM
Cards: MC V
Dress: Casual
Style: American $$

Menu Sampler: Kids Menu Too

Breakfast:
Eggs Benedict w/ham $8.45/$10.95, add vegetables $9.25/$11.25, Eggbert's Unique French Toast (until 11 AM) $5.95, French Omelette 2 eggs $4.25 or 3 eggs $5.65 with hash browns or toast, Denver Omelette with two eggs $8.75, with three eggs $9.95, Two Eggs, two pieces meat, rice or hash browns $6.95, Hotcakes $5.95, Pigs-In-A-Blanket two hotcakes around link sausages $6.25

Lunch:
BLT and chips $7.25, Fish Sandwich grilled in butter with chips $8.95, British Burger, ¼ # with bacon, American cheese, Thousand Island dressing, mac salad $8.75, The Big "O" an omelette sandwich with choice of ingredients $7.95, Pork and Cabbage $8.25, Bacon Mushroom Salad $8.25, Clam Chowder $3.95

Dinner:
You might consider going across the Coconut Marketplace to The Eggbert's sister restaurant, Hula Girl. Both have the same owner. The approach at Hula Girl is more upscale with entertainment and full bar service offered. Dinner was offered at The Eggbert's until recently when it was decided to stop duplicating their efforts and specialize on each restaurant's strengths. Call 808-822-4422.
Adult Beverages: N/A @ The Eggbert's, Beer/Wine/Cocktails @ Hula Girl

Impressions: Casual Cafe

The Eggbert's is an old Kauai institution. Long time visitors might remember it in Lihue before they made the move out to the Coconut Marketplace. Breakfast is the big draw with service until 3 PM. When were you last asked whether you wanted the eggs on your benedict prepared soft, medium or hard? After making that decision select your choice of toppings before adding the hollandaise sauce from heaven. The owners complete the day by serving an extensive lunch menu. This place specializes in serving mainland comfort food prepared a notch above.

Lihue

The Fish Express ✓✓

3343 Kuhio Hwy (Hwy 56)
Lihue, HI 96766
808-245-9918
Web: None
Hours: L 10:00 AM-3:00 PM
Market 10:00 AM-6:00 PM Mo-Sa
Market 10:00 AM-4:00 PM Su
Cards: MC V
Dress: Casual
Style: Fresh Fish/Local/Take-Out $

Menu Sampler:

Breakfast:
N/A
Lunch/Dinner:
Da Regulars: Served all-day-every-day Hawaiian Plate with choice of Laulau or Kalua, with a side of Lomi Salmon, choice of Poke and rice $7.50, Chinese Plate of Oriental Fried Chicken, Ginger Shrimp, Chop Suey, Spareribs and rice $7.95. Choice of Five Gourmet Bentos w/rice, nishime $4.95, Unagi Don $6.95
Fresh Fish Specials: Served Mo-Fr from 10-3, includes rice and a choice of potato salad or Nalo greens with Oriental wasabi dressing $7.95, Macadamia Nut Panko Crusted with Lilikoi Sauce, Grilled with Passion Orange Tarragon Sauce, Wok Seared with Thai Curry, Sautéed with Garlic and Herb Butter and side of tartar sauce, Blackened with Guava Basil, Katsu with Wasabi Cream
Fish & Stuff: Served Mo-Fr from 10-3, Fresh Fish Sandwich Grilled or Cajun, Fries $6.95, Fresh Fish Tacos two tacos with sour cream and guacamole $6.95, Stuffed Ahi Plate Ahi stuffed with crab & mushrooms & topped with a wasabi cream $7.95, Salmon Lumpia on Nalo greens with a Thai Chili Dressing $7.95
Adult Beverages: Beer

Impressions:

Takee Outee

Hawaii has establishments that can be viewed as the island equivalent of big city delis. These are the fish markets where all kinds of prepared foods are dished up as individual servings or by the pound. Since the local population is often Asian, fish and seafood hold sway where kosher meats might appear otherwise. Among these we know of none better than The Fish Express. This is a take out place that could pass muster with the pickiest of patrons. Those who have kitchens in their accommodations will be amazed at the affordability of the fresh fish. For the rest of us it's beach picnic heaven. Look across the highway from Lihue's Wal-Mart.

North Shore

The Hanalei Gourmet ✓✓

The Old School House at Hanalei Center
5-5161 Kuhio Hwy (Hwy 56)
Hanalei, HI 96714
808-826-2524
www.hanaleigourmet.com

Hours: L 10:30 AM-5:00 PM
D 5:00 PM-9:30 PM
Cards: AE DC DIS JCB MC V
Dress: Casual
Style: Café/Tropical Bar/Deli $$

Menu Sampler:

Kids Menu Too

Breakfast:
N/A
Lunch:
Primo Pupus: Asian Style Crab Cakes with chef's pineapple aioli sauce 9.50, Artichoke Dip with French baguette and breadsticks 9.50, Artichoke Toast 4.95
Salads: Roasted Garlic Caesar 5.95/8.95, Mediterranean Salad with feta cheese, balsamic vinaigrette and focaccia bread 8.50, Hanalei Waldorf of fresh greens, caramelized walnuts, fresh sliced apples, gorgonzola crumbles, house mango vinaigrette dressing 5.95/8.95, Chicken Salad Boat in a fresh papaya 8.95
Sandwiches: Oregon Bay Shrimp Sandwich with a New Orleans remoulade sauce 9.95, Dewey's Gorgonzola Burger with caramelized onions & fries 9.95
Dinner:
Pastas: Chicken Udon Stir Fry, mixed greens, focaccia bread 16.95, Shrimp Scampi, salad of mixed greens and focaccia bread 18.95, Pasta du Jour 16.95
Entrées: Beer Battered Fish & Chips with soy wasabi sauce, fries, Asian slaw $Market, Charbroiled Pork Chops with a spinach sauté 22.95, Mac Nut Fried Chicken with a guava lime sauce 19.95, Scallops Meuniere over croutes 22.95, Fresh Catch charbroiled, blackened or sautéed $Market, Charbroiled Rib Eye Steak seasoned w/Hawaiian salt and black pepper, garlic mushroom sauté 26.95
Adult Beverages: Beer/Wine/Cocktails – Corkage Fee 10.00

Impressions:

Bustling Tavern

Your first impression of this island favorite might be that you just wandered into a belly-up-to-the-bar hangout. That might be partially true, but there's a lot more to this unpretentious tavern than a shot-and-a-beer. Everyone from the line cook to the wait staff knows what they're doing. Back that up with an ambitious menu and complex preparations and you've got something you'd never expect up here.

East Coast

The Hukilau Lanai ✓✓✓

Kauai Coast Resort
520 Aleka Loop
Kapa'a, HI 96746
808-822-0600
www.gaylordskauai.com
Hours: D 5:00 PM-9:00 PM XMo
Cards: AE DC DIS JCB MC V
Dress: Resort Casual
Style: American/Pacific Rim $$$

Menu Sampler:

Kids Menu Too

Breakfast/Lunch:
N/A
Dinner:
Starters: Kona Lobster Curry Bisque 6.95, Sesame Chicken Salad 5.95, Sweet Potato Ravioli with Kilauea feta cheese and roasted Okinawan sweet potato in a lemon grass cream sauce 6.95, Kona Lobster & Goat Cheese Won Ton 9.95
Salads: Wally's Salad romaine, cucumber, tomato, bacon, red onion & citrus tossed with a savory papaya seed dressing 2.95/4.95, Beach Boy Caesar Salad 3.95/5.95, Kauai Kunana Dairy Chevre Salad greens tossed w/basil vinaigrette and garnished w/Kauai Kunana Dairy goat cheese & Kamuela tomato 4.94/6.95
Entrées: Oven Roasted Chicken with a shiitake mushroom veloute and basil red-skin mashed potatoes 15.95, Filet Mignon with Ulupalakua red wine sauce and tonight's special potato $Market, Sugar Cane Skewered Shrimp & Tropical Chicken Duet brushed with Dave's peanut barbeque sauce on orzo risotto 18.95
Desserts: Coconut Crème Caramel baked Big Island Vanilla Bean coconut custard in a pool of caramel sauce 5.95, Macadamia Nut Tart w/vanilla bean ice cream 7.95, Kauai Mocha Mousse Cake a dense chocolate mousse made with Kauai coffee and coated in ganache served on a decadent brownie crust 6.95
Food & Wine Tasting Menu: 5-6 PM Tu-Su, 6 courses with wines 40.00
Adult Beverages: Beer/Wine/Cocktails – Corkage Fee 10.00

Impressions:

Comfortably Upscale

This recent addition to the Kauai dining scene aims to please a variety of moods and tastes. On one hand the menu features old American favorites; while on the other diners can experience Pacific Rim cuisine. Meanwhile, the kitchen takes a page out of the Hawaii Regional Cuisine book through the extensive use of local products. This all comes together in a comfortable dining room where relaxing over dinner is the norm. Be sure to have reservations at this popular rendezvous.

South Shore

Tidepools ✓✓✓✓

Grand Hyatt Kauai Resort and Spa
1571 Poipu Road
Koloa, HI 96756
808-742-1234
www.kauai.hyatt.com
Hours: D 6:00 PM-10:00 PM
Cards: AE DC DIS JCB MC V
Dress: Resort Casual
Style: Contemporary Hawaiian $$$

Menu Sampler: Kids Menu Too

Breakfast/Lunch:
N/A

Dinner:
Appetizer: Thai Spiced Crab Cake & Ho'i'o Salad $15, Ahi Poke & Taro Chips $15, Grilled Ahi Tataki & Snapper Sashimi $15, Sugarcane Shrimp Cocktail $13, Seared Yuzu Scallops in Filo with red chili-papaya butter sauce $15
Soup & Salads: Coconut Lobster Cappuccino with Tahitian vanilla foam $8, Kawamata Tomato Salad, Maui Onions with Gorgonzola Balsamic Vinaigrette $9, Hawaiian Style Beef Ceviche with citrus shoyu and sesame wonton chips $14, Asian Chop Salad with Lobster and Kim Chee Vinaigrette $14
Entrées: Oven Roasted Ono crusted with banana and mac nuts, lilikoi ginger butter sauce $34, Seared Opah with blue crab and lobster, Tahitian Vanilla Hollandaise $36, Pineapple and Macadamia Nut Crusted Chicken Breast with mango-scallion rice, mountain apple-juniper cream $30, Grilled Beef Tenderloin with smashed Yukon potatoes, miso-gorgonzola butter and teriyaki demi glace $38, Garlic Peppercorn Rubbed Prime Rib, buttered Hamakua Mushroom Jus, Smashed Yukon Potatoes and Horseradish Cream Sauce $34
Adult Beverages: Beer/Wine Cellar/Cocktails – Corkage Fee Varies

Impressions: Romantic Dining

Tidepools is the signature restaurant of the Hyatt Regency Kauai Resort and Spa. Dining here means sitting under a thatched roof surrounded by bamboo décor, torches, and koi fishponds while the ocean surf pounds in the distance. This is truly an Old Hawaii setting. The wait staff presents the freshest island ingredients fused in creative preparations. A must try is the Coconut Lobster Cappuccino with Tahitian vanilla foam. Don't pass up the dessert offerings! This is an All-Hawaii personal favorite and would be a great choice for that romantic splurge night. Reservations are strongly recommended at all times.

Lihue

Tip Top Motel & Café ✓

3173 Akahi Street
Lihue, HI 96766
808-245-2333

Web: None
Hours: B 6:30 AM-11:30 AM XMo
L 11:00 AM-2:00 PM XMo
Cards: MC V
Dress: Casual
Style: American/Local/Japanese $

Menu Sampler:

Breakfast:
Ham & Cheese Omelet w/rice, hashbrowns or toast $7.25, Mac Nut, Banana or Pineapple Pancakes $4.15/$5.15 plus $.25 per topping, Oxtail Soup $9.00, Loco Moco $7.25, Sweet Bread French Toast $4.75, Fried Rice $2.00/$5.00, Soft Fried Noodles $5.50, Beef Stew $7.00, Bento of chicken, corned beef hash, teri meat, egg roll, Goteburg sausage, potato salad, pickled vegetables, rice $7.25, Grand Slam 2 pancakes, 2 eggs, choice of bacon, spam, ham or Portuguese sausage $9.95, add $.50 for Goteburg or smoked bacon, Miso soup $3.00

Lunch:
All entrées and daily specials are served with rice, mixed vegetables and potato or mac salad. Country Style Boneless Chicken $7.25, Chicken Wing Dings 7 pcs $7.00, Grilled Mahimahi $7.25, Honey Stung Chicken $7.25, Roast Pork $7.25, Hamburger Steak $7.25, Beef Cutlet $7.25, Teri Beef $7.25, Combo Specials w/ rice, mac salad and fried noodles $9.25/$9.75, Wun Tun Min w/vegetables $6.95, Saimin $5.00/$6.00, Chef Salad $6.75, Club Sandwich $4.75, Teri Sandwich $4.50, Hamburger $4.25, Bacon Cheeseburger $5.00, Tuna $3.50, Mahimahi Sandwich $4.75, Grilled Ham & Cheese $3.75, Shrimp Tempura $3.00/3pcs, French Fries $2.50, Tossed Salad $3.00, Assorted Beverages $1.50

Adult Beverages: N/A

Impressions:

Local Favorite

Are there motels in Hawaii? A few. Does this establishment cater primarily to locals? Sure does. Is the food good? It is. The Tip Top Café offers family kine dining in spotless surroundings. A visit to the Tip Top is a cultural experience. Local businessmen and groups of ladies as well as retirees and keiki gather in the roomy booths to enjoy the local cuisine and discuss all that's happening in Lihue. The menu follows suit offering traditional selections developed during Kauai's plantation era. This is a great choice for the comfortably adventurous.

West Side

Toi's Thai Kitchen ✓

Ele'ele Shopping Center
4469 Waialo Road
Ele'ele, HI 96705
808-335-3111
Web: None
Hours: L 10:30 AM-2:00 PM Tu-Sa
D 5:30 PM-9:00 PM Tu-Sa
Cards: MC V
Dress: Casual
Style: Thai $$

Menu Sampler:

Breakfast:
N/A
Lunch/Dinner:
Appetizers: Spring Rolls (6) with sweet and sour peanut sauce $7.95, Pork Wontons $7.00, Calamari Rings $7.00
Salads: Beef, Chicken or Pork Laab mixed with mint, Chinese parsley, green onions, ground rice, dry chilies and Toi's special Thai lime sauce (includes dessert) $10.95, Shrimp, Ono Fish, Calamari or Seafood Combo Salad with romaine, onions, cucumbers, tomatoes, parsley, mint (includes dessert) $12.95
Rice & Noodles: Tofu, Vegetarian, Pork, Beef or Chicken Pad Thai of stir-fried noodles with bean sprouts, green onions, sweet spices, ground peanuts $11.95
Soups: All served with rice, green papaya salad and dessert. Shrimp Tom Yum mild, medium or hot $13.95, Chicken Rice Soup with jasmine rice and garlic oil $10.95, Thai Saimin with tofu, vegetarian, pork, beef or chicken $7.95
Entrées: All entrées served with green papaya salad, dessert and choice of jasmine, sticky or brown rice. Toi's Chicken Satay with a creamy, spicy-sweet peanut sauce $13.95, Toi's Beef Ginger stir fried with heaps of fresh ginger $13.95, Seafood Combo Basil Delight $17.95, Chicken Matsaman Curry $13.95, Shrimp Red Curry $14.95, Tofu Yellow Curry $12.95
Adult Beverages: BYOB

Impressions:

Kauai Original

Ele'ele would never be mistaken for an urban center, but the hilltop shopping cluster in this unlikely location houses a comfortable little eatery serving solid Thai fare. Local legend has it that this was the first Thai eatery on Kauai. True or not, this place has been around as long as we can remember. Expect to find well-executed Thai specialties served in big portions at both lunch and dinner.

South Shore

Tomkats Grille ✓✓

5404 Old Koloa Road
Koloa, HI 96756
808-742-8887
Web: None
Hours: B 8:00 AM-10:45 AM
L 11:15 AM-5:00 PM
D 5:00 PM-9:30 PM
Cards: AE, MC, V
Dress: Casual
Style: Island/Pacific Fusion $$

Menu Sampler:

Kids Menu Too

Breakfast:
Three Egg Omelet $10.00, Uncle Bert's Steak & Eggs with 8 oz New York $16.00, Banana Mac Nut Pancakes $9.00, Loco Moco with two eggs $10.00
Lunch:
Homemade Kalua Pig Grilled Sandwich $8.00, Hot Pastrami $9.00, Local Style Roast Beef Sandwich $9.00, Mahi Mahi Sandwich $11.00, Paniolo Burgers $8.00-$9.00, Loco Moco plate lunch $10.00, Fish & Chips $15.00, all salads include toasted baguettes, Seafood Salad $11.00, Caesar Salad $7.00
Dinner:
South Side Seafood Pasta $17.00, 11 OZ. New York Steak $20.00, New York Steak & Shrimp Scampi $24.00, 1# King Crab Legs $Mkt, Paniolo Burgers & Sandwiches $8.00-$9.00, Hawaiian BBQ Pork Ribs $18.00, Fish Special of the Day w/salad & starch $20.00, Hawaiian Dinner $14.00, Loco Moco $10.00
Pupus:
11:15 AM-10:00 PM Seared Poke Bowl $9.00, Poipu Steamed Clams $10.00, Lemon Grass Grilled Shrimp $12.00, Buffalo Wings $8.00, Calamari $8.00
Adult Beverages: Beer/Wine Cellar/Cocktails – Corkage Fee $10.00

Impressions:

Massive Menu

This Old Koloa Town standard is the kind of place people revisit. Things start at breakfast before moving seamlessly through lunch to dinner. In the middle of all this there's a happy hour from 3-6 PM. If you miss part of it, the routine repeats itself seven days a week. Everything is backed by lengthy menus, large portions and affordable prices. It all happens on covered verandas spread around an open courtyard. If that's not enough we challenge you to bring somebody to the party who can't find something they'd like to order. This picture is that complete. The kids are also taken care of with affordable keiki menus offered at all mealtimes.

Kauai Dining

North Shore

Tropical Taco ✓✓

Halelea Building
5-5088 Kuhio Hwy (Hwy 56)
Hanalei, HI 96714
808-827-8226
www.tropicaltaco.com
Hours: L 11:00 AM-5:00 PM XSu
Cards: None
Dress: Casual
Style: Mexican $

Menu Sampler:

Breakfast:
N/A
Lunch/Dinner:
Tropical Taco deep fried or just warm $6.95, Tropical Fish Taco fish dipped in beer batter and fried golden brown or grilled $7.92, Fat Jack ten inches of flour tortilla with cheese, meat, beans, deep fried, topped with lettuce, salsa, cheese and sour cream $7.92, Fresh Fish Burrito of catch of the day fried and topped with the works of beans, lettuce, salsa, cheese and sour cream $6.96, Regular Taco $4.50, Veggie Burrito everything but the meat $5.76. Roger also added Taro Tacos made with taro grown behind his house for the adventurous types.
Adult Beverages: N/A

Impressions: One's Plenty

Roger and Barbara Kennedy would like to welcome you to their new taco eatery in Hanalei. For a look at its predecessor ask to see the old green panel van where it all began. In days gone by that truck was Roger's taco shop. Local legend has it that during a hurricane back in the early '90's, Roger chained his taco truck to a coconut tree in a desperate attempt to protect his investment and after donning a bicycle helmet rode out the storm inside. However, there's another version of this story that reports he hid inside the truck because it was safer than his house!

Eventually Roger surrendered to progress and relocated his operation in the new Halelea Building. In order to preserve the spirit of the original business, Roger's artistically inclined friends constructed a silhouette of the truck's side panel and mounted it on the wall between the kitchen and the dining room of his new taco palace. Now orders are placed and delivered through this "van window" as they always have been. Remember that these are tropical tacos created for Hawaiian size appetites. One will be more than enough for all but the hungriest teenagers.

East Coast

ver'de ✓✓

Kapa'a Shopping Center
4-1101 Kuhio Hwy (Hwy 56)
Kapa'a, HI 96746
808-821-1400
www.verdehawaii.com
Hours: 11:00AM-8:30PM XMoTu
Cards: MC V
Dress: Casual
Style: Mexican $/$$

Menu Sampler: Kids Menu Too

Breakfast:
N/A
Lunch/Dinner:
Greens & Pupus: Crispy Taco Salad with chile-lime dressing $8.99, Add red chile seared ahi or fresh catch $3.99, Seared Ahi Tostada w/Chimayo chile aioli & guacamole $10.99, ver'de Nacho w/beef short rib & Christmas chiles $6.99
Tacos: Fresh Catch Tacos $11.99, Plate $14.49, Al Pastor Chicharron Tacos "Street Vendor Style" $9.99, Plate $13.49, Any Three Tacos, Two Sides $17.99
Sopaipillas: Stuffed Sopaipillas w/choice of chile verde beef short rib or carne adovada, garlic papas, queso blanco, red or green sauce $9.99, Veggie Stuffed Sopaipillas & en salada $9.99, Sopaipillas With Honey $4.59
Burritos: Al Pastor & Chile ver'de Burrito with al pastor pork, garlic papas, pico de gallo, fresh cilantro, chile ver'de sauce & queso blanco $10.99; ver'de, ver'de Burrito with broccoli sautéed in chipotle, spinach, garlic papas $9.99, Carne Adovada "Red Pork" Burrito, garlic papas, choice of sauce $9.99
Hana Hou: ver'de, ver'de Chilaques w/veggies, egg $10.99, Huevos Rancheros $9.99, Local Loco-red chile scented sticky rice, beef short rib, egg $7.99
Sides: Choice of Two $3.99: Rice, Charro Beans, Ensalada de ver'de
Adult Beverages: Beer, Signature Cocktails, BYO - Corkage Fee $5.00

Impressions: Santa Fe Style

Regional preferences influence Mexican menus just like cuisines from any other large country. Here we find a variety created north of the border in New Mexico. This interpretation relies heavily on chiles and less on meat creating flavors that translate accurately regardless of the ingredients. A great example can be found in the use of sauces. Many dishes come with a choice of red, green or Christmas sauce. The latter is a combination of the first two and will be a pleasant surprise.

East Coast

Wahooo Seafood Grill & Bar ✓✓✓

4-733 Kuhio Hwy (Hwy 56)
Kapa'a, HI 96746
808-822-7833
Web: None
Hours: D 5:00 PM-9:00 PM
Cards: AE MC V
Dress: Resort Casual
Style: Neo Steak & Seafood $$$

Menu Sampler: Kids Menu Too

Breakfast:
N/A
Lunch: Teriyaki Grilled Chicken Sandwich with wasabi mayonnaise and french fries 9, Fresh Ahi Sandwich with fruit salsa and greens 11
Dinner:
Starters: Crab Stuffed Mushrooms 12, Braised Escargot 11, Steamed Clams in garlic butter champagne broth 12, Wok Fried Sashimi wrapped in nori 13
Soups & Salads: French Maui Onion with an essence of bay shrimp twist 10, Cioppino 23, Bouillabaisse 23, Ahi Poke 12, Blue Crab Meat Chowder 6/12
Steak & Seafood Combos: Any one item with your choice of Prime Rib OR Filet Mignon, Hawaiian Spiny Lobster Tail 49, King Crab Legs 45, Scampi 33
Entrées: Fresh Kampachi pan-fried then stuffed and baked with a special bay shrimp, cheese and spinach filling and port bordelaise 27, Papio (pompano) with Papillote of shrimp, scallops and mushrooms in a sherry cream sauce topped with asparagus 27, Lobster Saffron broiled, sliced and simmered in saffron butter 45, Seared Scallops with a lotus root passion fruit sesame glaze 23, 20 oz T-Bone 32, New York Sirloin 27, Roast Prime Rib of Beef 23/27, Filet Mignon Béarnaise 28, Shutome broiled with passion fruit glaze 26, Stuffed Pork Chops simmered in a Napa Valley Chardonnay 23, Teriyaki Rib Eye 25
Adult Beverages: Beer/Wine Cellar/Cocktails – Corkage Fee 15

Impressions: Leisurely Dining

Wahooo is a pleasant alternative to the usual Kapa'a dining venue. It's spacious, freestanding, and has an unhurried feel. The menu follows suit with an emphasis on casual fine dining. Read it over and you'll find complexity designed to create layers of flavor beyond that found in old time steak-and-seafood restaurants. We like to think of Wahooo as a place to spend the evening instead of just going out for dinner. From the vintage bamboo bar with its exotic drinks to the fresh island fish preps this establishment hits the mark. Think outside the box when ordering.

West Side

Waimea Brewing Co. ✓✓
Waimea Plantation Cottages
9400 Kaumualii Hwy (Hwy 50)
Waimea, HI 96796
808-338-9733
www.waimeabrewing.com
Hours: LD 11:00 AM-9:00 PM
Cards: AE DC DIS MC V
Dress: Casual
Style: American/Island $$

Menu Sampler:

Kids Menu Too

Breakfast:
N/A
Lunch/ Dinner:
Pupus: Ale Steamed Shrimp ½ # served with sweet Thai chili sauce $12.95, Nui Nachos $10.95, Taro Leaf Goat Cheese Dip with grilled pita bread $9.50
Salads: Asian Chicken Salad with citrus vinaigrette $10.95, Thai Beef $12.95
Sandwiches: all served with brewpub fries & Java slaw, Kalua Pork Sandwich pork roasted Hawaiian style topped with smoked provolone cheese on a Maui onion bun with lettuce, tomato and kosher pickle $10.95, Seared Poke Wrap with wasabi aioli and fresh veggies $11.95, Hawaiian Chicken Sandwich with slice of pineapple $9.75, Angus Beef Burger $8.95, Kalua Pork Wrap $9.50
Entrées: Kalua Pork on a bed of cabbage with kim chee and sticky rice $15.95, Jawaiian Chicken, Caribbean rice, black beans $15.95, Balsamic Glazed Strip Steak with wasabi mashed potatoes, veggies $19.95, Teriyaki Steak & Ale Shrimp wasabi mashed potatoes, veggies $29.95, Kalbi Beef Short Ribs sticky rice, veggies $18.95, Full Rack BBQ Ribs potatoes or rice, veggies $24.95
Brews: Wai'ale'ale Ale, Pakala Porter, Captain Cook's Original India Pale Ale, and Na Pali Pale Ale, West Side Wheat, Leilani Light, Cane Fire Red
Other Adult Beverages: Wine/Cocktails – Corkage Fee $10.00

Impressions:

Brew Pub

Want an unlikely scenario? How about coming across a brewpub in an old-time plantation village at the end of the highway in Waimea! The kitchen at Waimea Brewing Co. serves creative pupus and large servings of special sandwiches and entrées inside the pub or out on the veranda. It's easy to tell that the person who created the menu enjoyed the task. All manner of approaches and combinations appear to satisfy just about any foodies' fantasies. After sightseeing on the fiery west side the surprisingly good house crafted beers offer a great way to cool off.

West Side

Wrangler's Steakhouse ✓✓✓

9852 Kaumualii Hwy (Hwy 50)
Waimea, HI 96796
808-338-1218

Web: None
Hours: L 11:00 AM-4:00 PM Mo-Fr
D 5:30 PM-8:30 PM XSu
Cards: AE MC V
Dress: Casual
Style: Steak & Seafood $$$

Menu Sampler:

Kids Menu Too

Breakfast:
N/A

Lunch:
Chicken Caesar Salad with grilled chicken slices, greens and garlic toast $10.25, Shrimp Louis with bay shrimp, egg and fresh veggies $10.25, Wrangler Burger grilled steak patty with mushrooms, cheese, onions, sprouts and steak fries $9.25, Kau Kau Tin with beef teriyaki, tempura shrimp and veggies $9.95, Pulehu Steak of grilled New York Steak with special garlic sauce $14.50

Dinner:
Salads: Pistachio Crusted Salmon Salad $16.95, Bleu Cheese & Walnut $14.95
Entrées: include soup & salad bar, Grilled New York Cut served on a sizzling platter $28.00, Rib Eye with peppercorn sauce $24.00, Grilled Sirloin Steak & Scampi $30.00, Pork Chops with crispy sweet & sour onions $18.00, Steak & Lobster Tail $Mkt, New York Steak with zucchini, mushroom, onion & caper sauté $25.00, Steak & King Crab Legs $32.00, Ahi with penne pasta, vegetables, bell pepper sauce $18.00, Scampi with linguini with garlic cream sauce $18.00
Desserts: Warm Peach Cobbler w/vanilla bean ice cream $5.50, Flan $5.50
Adult Beverages: Beer/Wine/Cocktails – Corkage Fee $10.00

Impressions:

Solid Choice

Wrangler's Steakhouse is located in the last town you pass through when driving to the Waimea Canyon. This restaurant is a wonderful addition to the west shore dining scene. It combines the area's picturesque past with a contemporary menu. Better yet, they do it at lunch as well as dinner. The central focus might be steak and seafood, but it's done with flair and offers some local culinary treats as well. Expect to find a well conceived collection of properly prepared dishes served by a cheerful wait staff. Those on the move might want to consider the pizza palace next door. It belongs to the same people and maintains similarly high standards.

KAUAI DINING BY REGION

Kauai Dining By Region

West Side

South Shore

Lihue

East Coast

North Shore

HAWAII
FOOD & CULTURE
GLOSSARY

Hawaii Food & Culture Glossary

a'a	rough clinker lava
aina	the land
abalone	large saltwater mollusk
aburage	deep-fried tofu
adobo	marinated Filipino chicken and/or pork stew
agemono	Japanese cooking method of preparing meats and vegetables by deep-frying
ahi	yellowfin tuna, often served raw as sashimi on a bed of Chinese cabbage with a wasabi and shoyu dipping sauce
ahupua'a	a land division used in old Hawaii consisting of all the lands between two adjoining ridges from the top of the mountain to the ocean
akamai	clever or smart
akua	spirit or god
ali'i	chief or noble
aloha	versatile term that can mean hello, good-bye, and love
Aloha Friday	casual dress day or more importantly the first day of the weekend party that actually starts Thursday afternoon
arroz	rice
arugula	peppery flavored greens
aumakua	guardian spirit
auntie	any older lady, a term of respect

'awa	kava, a beverage made from the ground roots of the intoxicating pepper
azuki	red beans
banh hoi	Vietnamese meat and vegetable roll-up
barbecue stick	char grilled teriyaki meat stick
bean curd	tofu
bean threads	fine thin noodles made from mung bean starch, long rice
bento	Japanese box lunch
black beans	fermented beans used in Chinese sauces
bok choy	a tall variety of cabbage with white celery like stems and dark green leaves
bulgoki	Korean teriyaki barbecue beef
bun	thin soft Vietnamese rice noodles
butterfish	black cod, has a smooth silky texture
carne	meat
cascaron	Filipino fried sweet dumpling
char siu	sweet marinated barbecued pork
chili oil	liquid fire made from chili peppers and oil
Chinese cabbage	a compact variety of cabbage with white celery-like stems and pale green leaves, also known as Napa cabbage or won bok
chorizo	hot and spicy sausage
chow	stir-fry
chow fun	cooked noodles combined with green onions and bits of meat or seafood then stir-fried with sesame oil

chun	Korean method of frying using flour followed by an egg wash
cilantro	Chinese parsley
coconut creme	thick creamy layer on top of a can of coconut milk
coconut milk	liquid extracted by squeezing grated coconut meat
crack seed	sweet or sour snack foods made from preserved fruits and seeds
da kine	what-cha-ma-call-it
daikon	large white Asian root vegetable commonly used as a garnish
dashi	broth made from dried seaweed and flakes of dried bonito
Diamond Head	directional term used on Oahu meaning to go east in the direction of Diamond Head or "Go Diamond Head"
dim sum	Chinese style dumplings
doce	sweet
donburi	thinly sliced meat, vegetables, and coddled egg served in a deep bowl over rice
edamame	lightly salted and boiled young soybeans
egg roll	fried pastry roll with various meat and vegetable fillings
Ewa	directional term used on Oahu meaning to go west in the direction of Ewa or "Go Ewa" which is opposite from Diamond Head and toward Pearl Harbor
fish cake	ground white fish, starch, and salt cooked together by steaming or frying
fish sauce	potent seasoning made from salt and fish

five spice powder	mixture of several spices that usually includes fennel, peppercorns, cinnamon, cloves, and star anise.
furikake	a dry condiment used on rice dishes
fusion cuisine	layers of flavor, texture, temperatures, and techniques created by combining elements from the cuisines of different cultures
ginger	spicy pungent root vegetable used as a flavoring in Asian cooking
gobo	burdock root
grinds	food
guava	sweet red tropical fruit
guisates	Filipino pork or chicken dish made with peas and pimento in a tomato based sauce
hale	house or building
halo halo	tropical fruit sundae made with ice, milk and sugar instead of ice cream, to mix - mix
ham har	fermented dried shrimp paste, very funky, a little goes a long way
hana	work
hana hou	do it one more time/encore!
haole	Caucasian
hapa	half as in hapa-haole or half-Caucasian
haupia	coconut custard dessert
Hawaii Regional Cuisine	movement started in the late '80's/early '90's by young local chefs combining island cooking styles and classic techniques with fresh local products to create an exciting new fusion cuisine

Hawaiian chili water	liquid heat made with Hawaiian chili peppers, water, and salt
Hawaiian rock salt	coarse white or pink rock salt
Hawaiian time	later rather than sooner
heiau	ancient Hawaiian stone temple
hekka	a stir-fry dish made with meat and vegetables in a shoyu-based sauce
hibachi	small charcoal cooker
hoisin sauce	thick, sweet, but pungent sauce used in Chinese cooking
holoholo	pleasure trip, to go "holoholo"
hono	bay
honu	turtle
hukilau	pulling of a large fish net by a group
hui	club or association
hula	Hawaiian native dance
huli huli	"turn turn" as in grilling chicken
imu	Hawaiian underground oven made by digging a pit and lining it with hot lava rocks covered by banana plants and food and burying it for several hours, used at luaus for making kalua pork, laulau, sweet potatoes, etc.
inari sushi	cone sushi made by filling fried tofu pockets with sweet vinegar flavored rice
ipo	sweetheart
kaffir lime leaves	leaves of the kaffir lime tree used as flavoring in Thai cooking

kahuna	priest or skilled person
kai	the sea
kaiseki	Japanese fine dining in courses
kal bi ribs	Korean teriyaki beef short ribs
kale	Portuguese cabbage
kalo	taro
kalua pork	shredded pork prepared luau style in an imu pit, also known locally as kalua pig
kama'aina	long time resident or someone who was born in Hawaii
kamaboko	Japanese fish cake
kane	man
kapu	forbidden
kapuna	grandparent or wise older person
katsu	breaded cutlet
kau kau	food, a place to eat
keiki	child
kiawe	dry land hardwood used in smoking and grilling meats
ki'i	statue or image
kim chee	spicy Korean condiment made from fermented cabbage and peppers
koa	valuable hardwood tree, warrior
Koko Head	directional term used on Oahu meaning to go in the direction of Koko Head or "Go Koko Head"
kokua	help

kona	leeward
kona wind	muggy airflow from the equator
kukui	candlenut tree, the source of kukui nut oil
Kula	a truck gardening district in Upcountry Maui
kulolo	sweet pudding made with poi
kumu	teacher as in kumu hula
lanai	deck or patio
lau hala	woven mats
lau lau	flavored meat mixed with taro leaves and wrapped in ti leaves then steamed, often in an imu
laver	purple seaweed used in making nori
lechon	roasted pig
lei	garland of flowers
lemon grass	woody lemon flavored grass used as flavoring in Southeast Asian cooking
li hing mui	sweet and sour seasoning made from dried plums and salt
lilikoi	passion fruit
limu	edible seaweed
linguica	spicy Portuguese pork sausage seasoned with garlic and paprika
loa	long
loco moco	local dish consisting of rice, a large hamburger patty or slices of Spam, and fried eggs with lots of brown gravy over all
lolo	crazy

lomi	to knead or massage
lomi lomi salmon	salted salmon finely diced with tomatoes and green onions
long rice	clear noodles cooked in broth
lua	restroom
luau	Hawaiian feast, also a dish made from taro leaves, coconut crème, and meat
lulu	calm
lumpia	fried spring roll with meat, vegetable, or dessert fillings
lup cheong	Chinese pork sausage
lychee	sweet white fruit
macadamia nuts	small round nut with creamy but crunchy texture
mac salad	macaroni and mayonnaise
mahalo	thank you
mainland	North America
makai	directional term that is helpful on an island meaning to turn or look toward the ocean
maki sushi	sushi rolled in nori
malasada	wonderful sweet brought here by the Portuguese similar to a fresh sugar donut but minus the hole
malihini	newcomer
malo	loincloth
mana	power or energy from the spirit world
manapua	steamed pork bun

mandoo	Korean dumplings with meat and vegetable fillings
mango	golden fleshed tropical fruit
mano	shark
Manoa	a gardening district near Honolulu, the Manoa Valley
mauka	directional term meaning to look or turn toward the mountain or uphill part of an island
mauna	mountain
mein	Chinese noodles
mele	chant or song
menehune	legendary "little people" of Hawaii
mirin	sweet rice cooking wine
miso	fermented soybean paste
miso soup	light Japanese soup made from soybean paste and garnished with tofu, kamaboko, daikon, green onions, and wakame
mixed plate	plate lunch version of a mixed grill
moa	native Polynesian chicken
moana	ocean
mochi	rice cake
mochiko	sweet rice flour
mo'o	lizard or water spirit
musubi	rice ball
muu muu	loose fitting ankle length dress

naan	Indian flatbread
nabemono	Japanese cooking method of preparing thin slices of meat and vegetables in a hot broth
'Nalo	As in Waimanalo, a garden district on the Windward side of Oahu
nam pla	Thai fish sauce
nam prik	Thai hot sauce
nani	beautiful
nene	Hawaiian goose
nigiri sushi	oblong sushi
niu	coconut
noni	native shrub bearing medicinal fruit
nori	roasted seaweed pressed into sheets
norimaki	sushi rolled in nori
nui	big or great
nuoc mam	Vietnamese fish sauce
off-island	in the islands one does not go "out of town" they go "off-island"
ogo	type of seaweed favored by the Japanese
ohana	extended family
ohelo	native shrub bearing edible berries
okazuya	a Japanese delicatessen where fast foods and snacks are served buffet style
ono	delicious
opae	shrimp

opihi	Hawaiian escargot harvested from rocks along the ocean and eaten raw with salt
oyster sauce	thick brown sauce made from oysters and shoyu often used in stir fry dishes
Pacific Rim Cuisine	a fusion of cuisines involving methods and ingredients from the countries around the Pacific Ocean
pad thai	Thai noodles
pahoehoe	smooth ropey lava
pakalolo	crazy smoke, marijuana, buds; something to decline when offered
pali	cliff
pancit	Filipino noodles
paniolo	Hawaiian cowboy
panko	Japanese breadcrumbs
pao	bread
pao doce	Portuguese sweet bread
papaya	smooth skinned orange-fleshed tropical fruit that can also be used green when peeled and shredded in a salad
pasteles	similar to a tamale except made with bananas instead of corn flour
patis	Filipino fish sauce
pau	finished
pau hana	finished working
pho	Vietnamese noodle soup
pidgin	Hawaiian Creole English
pipi kaula	Hawaiian beef jerky

plantain	cooking banana
plate lunch	island style blue plate special with a main entrée such as teriyaki beef or chicken, two scoops of white rice, and a scoop of macaroni salad
poi	glutinous paste made by pounding steamed taro root, the Hawaiian staple starch
poke	ceviche dish made with cubed fish or sliced octopus mixed with onion and seaweed then marinated in shoyu and spices
pono	righteous
ponzu	tart Japanese citrus sauce
Portuguese sausage	spicy garlic and paprika flavored pork sausage, linguica
pua	flower
pua'a	pig
pueo	owl
puka	hole
pupu	appetizer
pu'u	hill
ramen	curly Japanese wheat noodles
rice noodle	noodles made with rice flour
rice paper	round rice flour wrapper that is soaked in hot water to soften before use
saimin	island noodle soup that has many variations and broths--extras may include Spam, teriyaki beef, green onions, vegetables, hard-cooked eggs, and fish cake

sake	Japanese rice wine
sashimi	raw fish sliced very thin and served with spicy condiments and dipping sauce
satay	tender chicken or beef strips marinated in coconut milk and spices then skewered and grilled
sesame oil	aromatic oil made from sesame seeds used sparingly to flavor Asian dishes
shabu shabu	chafing dish cookery involving thinly sliced meats and vegetables simmered in broth usually with a tabletop preparation
shaka	hand signal using the thumb and little finger used as a greeting
shave ice	similar to a snow cone except there is no crunch as the ice is shaved instead of crushed, can be topped with wonderful tropical flavored syrups and served with ice cream and azuki beans
shoyu	Japanese soy sauce, Aloha Brand is preferred in the islands as it is not as salty as some other types
soba	Japanese buckwheat noodles
somen	thin Japanese wheat noodles
Spam	canned spiced pork lunchmeat
spring roll	fried rice paper roll with various fillings
starch	rice or potatoes
sukiyaki	Japanese beef, tofu, vegetable, and noodle dish with shoyu based sauce commonly cooked at the table
summer roll	fresh rice paper roll with various fillings
sushi	small slices of vegetables, fruits, fish, or meat combined with tangy rice

sweet bread	rich egg bread commonly called Molokai or Portuguese sweet bread
sweet rice	also known as sticky rice or glutinous rice
tako	octopus
talk story	to have a casual conversation
tapa	cloth made from pounded tree bark
taro	starchy root plant used in making poi
teri	teriyaki
teishoku	a complete Japanese meal including soup, salad, entrée, pickled vegetables, and rice
tempura	meat, seafood, or vegetables fried in a light batter coating
tendon	meat and vegetable tempura served over rice
teppanyaki	Japanese cooking method of grilling vegetables, seafood, meat and rice tableside by a knife-wielding chef, very entertaining
teriyaki	sweet tangy shoyu based marinade
Thai basil	herb used in Thai cooking, has a purple flower and sharper taste than sweet basil
ti	broad-leafed plant whose leaves are used for plates, hula skirts, and for wrapping foods and religious offerings
tobiko	flying fish roe, caviar
tofu	soybean curd available fresh or fermented
tom yum	spicy Thai soup
tonkatsu	fried cutlet
tsukemono	pickled vegetables

tuong ot — Vietnamese hot sauce

tutu — grandmother

two scoop rice — two scoops of cooked white rice

uala — sweet potato

udon — thick Japanese wheat noodles

ulu — breadfruit

vertical food — a physical manifestation of fusion cuisine where the elements of the dish are stacked

wahine — woman

wai — water

wakame — a seaweed condiment

wasabi — spicy Japanese horseradish paste often combined sparingly with shoyu to make a dipping sauce for sushi and sashimi

wiki wiki — hurry up, very fast

wok — round bottomed cooking pot used over very high heat to quick sear or stir-fry chopped meats and vegetables

won bok — Chinese cabbage

won ton — Chinese meat dumplings

wor — vegetables

yakimono — Japanese cooking method of preparing meats and vegetables by broiling or grilling

yakiniku — tabletop grilling

yakisoba — grilled noodles

yakitori — grilled meat and vegetable kebabs

HAWAII FISH & SEAFOOD GLOSSARY

Hawaii Fish & Seafood Glossary

Hawaii IS the island state, and what could be a more fitting centerpiece on a Hawaiian menu than the bounty of the sea? Just like everything else found in this Pacific paradise there are unique spins to the fish and seafood selections. With this in mind we have created a separate glossary to help you explore and better appreciate the aquatic offerings found in Hawaii's dining spots.

Visitors need to be aware that finfish are nearly always listed by their Hawaiian names on island menus. That's no problem for those who grew up in Hawaii, but the rest of us would do well to brush up on the subject first. How else would you know that an ahi is a big eye or yellow fin tuna, and that a tako is definitely not the same as a taco? The word tako in Hawaii means octopus and receiving one instead of the other could come as quite a surprise!

Most people don't realize that longliners stay out for several days at a time, but trollers come in every night and that the difference in the quality and freshness of their catch can be noticed. If you are paying for fresh island fish you want to make sure that you get it. You might see the term day boat used in some of the finer restaurants to describe the freshest of fresh fish and seafood. Regardless, make sure to ask and always insist on fish that has never been frozen.

As long as we're on the subject of getting what you're paying for, let's take a look at the economics of fish and seafood in Hawaii. There's a misconception that just because people see "water, water everywhere", the aquatic resources must be limitless and their prices low. Nothing could be farther from the truth. The high cost of production through aquaculture and harvest in the wild along with huge local and foreign demand drive prices to the upper limit of the menu.

In closing, when you decide to take the plunge and go out for fish or seafood, make it a point to trust the recommendations at the restaurant. The chef knows how to match species and preparations for the best possible results. Just let your waiter know what you have in mind and listen to his suggestions. You'll be far happier in the end if you go with the flow than if you try to have it your way.

ahi — big eye or yellow fin tuna

aku — skipjack tuna, most common spring through early fall, robust flavor, firm texture, often served as poke or in sushi, primarily caught by commercial pole-and-line fishermen and recreational trollers

akule — big-eyed scad, a local favorite, primarily caught by netting or by hook-and-line fishermen

ama ebi	sweet shrimp or langoustines, harvested with traps from deep water, available locally but often imported
a'u	billfish of any type
big eye ahi	big eye tuna, most common from mid-fall through mid-spring, moderate beef-like flavor, medium firm texture, favored for sashimi and poke, primarily caught by long-line boats
ehu	red snapper, moderate flavor, most common during winter, medium firm texture, primarily caught by deepwater hook-and-line fishermen
hapu'upu'u	grouper or sea bass, most common spring and fall, moderate flavor, medium firm texture, primarily caught by deepwater hook-and-line fishermen
hebi	shortbill spearfish, most common mid-spring through early fall, moderate flavor, medium firm texture, primarily caught by commercial long-line boats
kajiki	pacific blue marlin, most common summer through fall, moderate flavor, firm texture, primarily caught by commercial long-line boats and recreational trollers
Keahole lobster	clawed "Maine" lobsters raised on the Big Island through aquaculture, available all year
Kona lobster	spiny or rock lobster, primarily caught by divers working the reef or by trapping, usually imported, available all year
lehi	silver mouth snapper, most common during late fall and winter, moderate flavor, medium texture, primarily caught by deepwater hook-and-line fishermen

mahimahi dolphinfish, most common spring and fall, moderate almost sweet flavor, medium texture, ask if the fish is fresh "island fish", primarily caught by commercial and recreational trollers

moi pacific threadfin, the royal fish, now raised locally through aquaculture, mild flavor, delicate texture, available all year

monchong bigscale or sickle pomfret, available all year, robust flavor, medium firm texture, primarily caught as a by-catch of tuna long-liners and deepwater hook-and-line fishermen.

nairagi striped marlin, most common winter and spring, moderate flavor, medium firm texture, primarily caught by commercial long-line boats and recreational trollers

onaga ruby or long-tailed red snapper, most common late fall and winter, mild flavor, medium texture, primarily caught by deepwater hook-and-line fishermen

ono wahoo, most common late spring through early fall, mild almost citrus-like flavor, medium firm texture, primarily caught by commercial and recreational trollers with part of the catch harvested by commercial long-line fishermen

opae shrimp, now raised locally through aquaculture, available all year

opah moonfish, most common spring through summer, robust flavor, medium texture, primarily caught by commercial long-line fishermen fishing over seamounts

opakapaka crimson snapper, most common fall and winter, mild flavor, delicate texture, primarily caught by deepwater hook-and-line fishermen

opihi	small limpet, found on coastal rock faces in the surf zone, eaten raw with salt as "Hawaiian escargot"
papio	juvenile pompano or crevally, medium flavor, firm texture, caught by shore casters, shallow water trollers, and bottom fishermen
shutome	broadbill swordfish, most common spring and summer, moderate flavor, medium firm texture, caught at night by commercial long-line fishermen
tako	octopus or squid, primarily caught by divers working in shallow water or by jigging
tombo	albacore or "white meat" tuna, most common mid-spring through mid-fall, moderate flavor, medium texture, primarily caught by commercial long-line fishermen and small-boat hand line fishermen
uku	grey snapper, most common mid-spring through mid-fall, moderate flavor, medium firm texture, primarily caught in deep water by hook-and-line fishermen but is also caught near the surface by recreational trollers
ula	spiny or rock lobster, primarily caught by divers working the reef or by trapping
ula papapa	slipper lobster, primarily caught by divers working the reef or by trapping
ulua	adult pompano or crevally, medium flavor, firm texture, caught by shore casters, shallow water trollers, and bottom fishermen
yellow fin ahi	yellow fin tuna, most common mid-spring through mid-fall, moderate beef-like flavor, medium firm texture, favored for sashimi and poke, primarily caught by commercial long-line boats and commercial and recreational trollers

Hawaii Restaurant Guide Series

Kauai Restaurants And Dining
With Princeville And Poipu Beach
ISBN 1-931752-37-0 $8.95 US

Maui Restaurants And Dining
With Lanai And Molokai
ISBN 1-931752-38-9 $9.95 US

Oahu Restaurants And Dining
With Honolulu And Waikiki
ISBN 1-931752-39-7 $9.95 US

Big Island Of Hawaii Restaurants And Dining
With Hilo And The Kona Coast
ISBN 1-931752-40-0 $8.95 US

Hawaii Budget Restaurants And Dining
With All Six Hawaiian Islands
ISBN 1-931752-41-9 $8.95 US

Individual Orders Can Be Placed Through All Major Book Retailers. Inquiries On Wholesale Or Quantity Orders Can Be Sent To The Ingram Book Company

-Or-

Holiday Publishing Inc
PO Box 11120
Lahaina, HI 96761

holidaypublishing@yahoo.com
www.hawaiirestaurantguide.com

LaVergne, TN USA
30 June 2010
187897LV00008B/55/P

9 781931 752374